COURAGE
at Indian Deep

COURAGE
at Indian Deep

JANE RESH THOMAS

CLARION BOOKS
New York

For my mother, THELMA SCOTT RESH
I had a mother who read to me.

Clarion Books
a Houghton Mifflin Company imprint
215 Park Avenue South, New York, NY 10003

Copyright © 1984 by Jane Resh Thomas
All rights reserved.
For information about permission to reproduce
selections from this book, write to Permissions,
Houghton Mifflin Company, 2 Park Street, Boston, MA 02108
Printed in the USA

Library of Congress Cataloging in Publication Data
Thomas, Jane Resh.
Courage at Indian Deep.
Summary: Forced to move to northern Minnesota from
a comfortable life in Minneapolis, a family finds the
need to make some big adjustments.
[1. Moving, Household—Fiction.   2. Minnesota—
Fiction]   I. Title.
PZ7.T36695Cp   1984   [Fic]   83-14404
PA ISBN 0-395-55699-6   ISBN 0-89919-181-9

AGM 10 9 8 7 6 5 4 3 2 1

Author's Note

I have been in love with the wondrous power and beauty of the Great Lakes all my life. In childhood, I fished with my father off the pier at Saugatuck, on Lake Michigan, where some of my relatives drowned when their ship "cracked like an eggshell" in a storm. My grandfather, Arthur Oliver Scott, used to tell me a story about the time in 1895 when he stood on a high bluff overlooking Lake Michigan and saw the *Chicora* founder in heavy seas and go down with all hands. He was a boy, and the men he begged for help scoffed at his account. The *Chicora* and its sailors were never heard from again. This book grew out of my memory of that old story, blended with imaginary events, tales of heroic rescues on the Great Lakes, and stories friends tell about their own lives on the North Shore of Lake Superior.

One

The bears had not yet lumbered out of the dusky woods for their regular feast, but a trio of gulls cackled in a dead pine tree. Here on the east side of the mountain the sun was down.

Turning off the ignition and letting the old car coast down the hill to the entrance of the county dump, Mrs. Kennedy explained softly to her children, "If this rattletrap burps, it'll scare away the evening's entertainment."

"Remember when we saw the old bear with two cubs in that tree over there?" whispered the girl, Eileen, as she searched the clearing through the windshield.

"Of course I remember," said her younger brother, Cass, from the back seat. "That was only a month ago. Roll up your window, Eileen. I have nightmares about bears grabbing me."

Tongue stepped on Cass, wagging his whole body, not just his tail. True to his name, the old black Labrador dog gave Cass a wet swipe across the side

1

of his face. The boy buried his cheek in his dog's fat neck.

"He's got a tick behind his ear, Mom," Cass said.

"We'll take it off when we get home."

Cass pressed his face against the window and breathed a patch of fog on the glass as he strained to see. He wanted to be first to notice a black shadow detach itself from the mist and gloom at the forest's edge and reveal itself as a bear. "Tongue never got ticks when we lived in Minneapolis," he said.

"Of course not," his mother replied. "He was always penned up in our little backyard."

"That's how Cass always talks to the kids at school," said Eileen furiously. "You'd think Minneapolis was paradise."

"Even this place might be paradise if the kids weren't so dumb," Cass said. "Ansel Peterson's the only one who lives close enough, and he lords it over me just because I didn't grow up in a shack in the woods. Or in a tavern, like him."

Cass watched the smudgy smoke rise from a small fire at one end of the pit, the source, he guessed, of the acrid stench that smelled worse than garbage.

"You ought to hear Cass on the school bus, bragging about the things he did back home." Eileen struck a pose. "He worked backstage at the Children's Theatre," she said in a haughty rising voice.

"Shh!" whispered Cass. "You'll scare the bears."

"He acts like such a snob," she hissed. "He told Ansel Peterson that he and Dad are going to hunt bear with pistols this fall. Everybody laughs at him."

"Shut up," Cass shouted, grabbing Eileen's arm. Although at twelve she was a year older, they were the same size, and Cass was stronger. He could win, he knew.

Mom firmly separated their hands, her dark eyes smoldering. She looked like a larger version of Eileen, with her hair pulled back in a thick black braid that hung coiled in the hood of her navy sweatshirt. But worry lines around her eyes had deepened in the past year.

"Since we're all in the same boat, your self-pity does get tiresome, Cass," she said.

He watched the woods, refusing to meet her eyes, but he could see Tongue growing restless, glancing from one to the other.

"When the school board closed those eighteen schools last year, your dad had taught chemistry for fourteen years." She spoke with the force that dammed-up anger always has. "Do you think he *chose* to be a state trooper up here and run our dinky resort?"

"He could have found another job back home," said Cass, seeing his mother's anger but goading her anyway.

"Have some mercy, Cass! There *were* no other jobs. He only got this one because he was a policeman before he went to college."

Tin cans rattling down the side of the pit flushed a pair of crows, which fluttered up and then settled

3

back to their work. One of them carried a strip of ragged paper in its beak like a shabby banner. Herring gulls, so graceful in the air, waddled among the garbage that was strewn in the grass and bushes.

"Can't you see? He's back where he started," Mom went on in a more patient voice, "but he's lucky to have any kind of job. Teachers all over the state are out of work."

She sighed. "It's been a hard year for all of us."

Tongue growled low in his chest.

Eileen, who had pulled her hood up over her head and tied it firmly under her chin when Mom entered the argument, whispered, "Shh! I saw one. There's another!"

Out of the mist on the other side of the clearing, moving shapes materialized, as black as the mouth of night. Three of them, then a fourth, came toward the garbage pit, swaying rhythmically, raising majestic heads to smell the wind, brushing the ground with their broad paws.

They looked as if they owned the world.

Then the bears descended into the pit, their rounded backsides bouncing comically. There they sat on their haunches, no longer majestic, and began to root in the garbage.

Tongue sniffed and tried to see. Suddenly a man stepped out from behind a rusting kitchen stove, downwind from the animals, Cass noticed. The startled bears jumped back farther into the pit, making the cans and old lawn chairs clatter. The man approached the grassy edge, shooting pictures in the dusk with a flash attachment on his camera.

"They could knock him flat with their eyes closed," whispered Cass, amazed by the man's stupidity.

But the bears had already turned again to their dinner. Ignoring the man, they ripped plastic trash bags with claws adapted for digging insects out of tree trunks, nosed through rotten food, and sorted the junk and broken bottles and jagged tin cans, looking for table scraps.

"If flashbulbs don't faze them," said Cass, "why are we whispering?"

"Isn't it sickening?" said Eileen. "Why do they lower themselves?"

"Because they're hungry," said Mom.

The smallest of the bears plunged its head into a gallon mayonnaise jar and then couldn't get out. It stood on its hind legs, clownish and ridiculous, struggling to pull the jar off its head. Thrashing about, it lost its balance and fell against a rusty oil drum. The glass shattered. The bear shook its head and rubbed its ears. Then it ran lickety-split back into the mist and the darkness.

All the while the man kept taking pictures, as if the bears were his playthings, Cass thought, and this clearing in the woods the worst kind of zoo.

"I can't stand this," Cass groaned. "Let's get out of here."

"Now you can see why I can't get excited when you kids want to come up here," Mom said. She had

5

already started the car and pulled away, but around a bend in the road, she had to wait while a woman maneuvered a big pink car which blocked the exit gate.

"Tourists like them come here to the North Shore because they 'love' the place," said Mom with scorn, "but they want to pave the woods and pet the wild animals. You're upset because that man has no respect."

Edging around the car, Mom drove on. "And the bears have lost their own self-respect," she said, "but they're still dangerous. That's why the county is going to padlock this place."

"They ought to protect the bears," said Cass. "It's the people who are dangerous."

As they drove down the steep hills which are the eroded remains of the prehistoric Sawtooth Mountains, Lake Superior shone like chrome in the failing sunlight. They could see an ore boat steaming toward the depot where iron ore was shipped to steel mills in the East.

"What do you say we stop at the harbor?" said Mom.

"Yeah," said Eileen, "the wind will wash the smell of garbage out of my nose."

"Let's never go back there," said Cass.

They turned off the highway and followed the gravel road behind the Mesabi Shipping Company's garages. Mom paused by the playing field to watch a football sail through the dusk and two teams of boys charge toward the far goalposts. A cheer arose from the crowd of parents whose cars and pickup trucks were parked beside the road.

"Why don't you join the football team, Cass?" said Mom. "That would help you make friends with the other boys."

"Ansel's the captain. Unlike the bears," Cass said sarcastically, "I'm not that hard up."

Mom closed her lips in a hard line and gave Cass a disgusted look as she released the hand brake. She started the car again and headed down to the parking lot on the shore, where tourists watched the ore boats being loaded.

"We're just in time," said Eileen. "It's the *A. O. Scott.*"

"And there's the *Madge* out there waiting to come in," said Mom.

She pulled up beside the only other car in the lot, an old gray sedan with a very shiny finish. Three white-haired women and a man sat inside, watching the ship through closed windows. The lady in the front seat was wiping the steam off the windshield with a handkerchief.

"They're the people who rented Cabin 1," said Mom. Cass and Eileen got out, pulling their necks into their sweatshirts in the harbor's cold wind. Cold weather came early here on the edge of the northern wilderness, and stayed late in the spring. Even now, at the end of September, the temperature fell below freezing at night.

"Look. You can see your breath." Eileen blew puffs into the air above her head. "Ansel Peterson can blow rings without even smoking."

Cass walked away angrily and climbed the rock ledge where he liked to sit and watch the ore boats steam by. Tongue rushed past, clambered up ahead of him, and sat down on his haunches, sniffing the air. Cass looked up at the freight train that was slowly crossing the trestle high above the boat. As each railway car reached a point at the center of the trestle, its bottom opened and its load of taconite emptied into enormous storage bins that stood at the edge of the water.

The falling ore thundered continuously; a cloud of red dust rose high above the train and hung in the air. Cass was counting the cars as they passed the drop point when somebody behind him said, "Hey, hotshot, this is my rock!"

He turned and saw Ansel Peterson too late to defend himself. In one smooth motion, Ansel kicked him between the shoulder blades and shoved him off the rock. Although the fall knocked the wind out of him, Cass saw fear wipe the malicious smile off Ansel's face.

Tongue had whirled, snarling. As Cass jumped to his feet, Tongue chased the boy off the other side of the rock into the parking lot, and Mom chased Tongue, shouting commands. The dog came back triumphantly with a big piece of blue denim in his mouth, which he dropped like a trophy at Cass's feet. Two other boys in football jerseys were watching at a distance. When Eileen grabbed Tongue's red collar to put him in the car, they ran away after Ansel.

"I take it the football game is over," Mom said wryly. "No wonder you don't like football."

Cass flinched as she put her arm around his bruised shoulder and brushed the dust off his sweatshirt. "What a mean trick," she said. "Is he always so nasty?"

"Always," said Cass. He wrenched himself away from his mother's tenderness and climbed the rock wall again. She watched him for a moment and then turned to join Eileen at the harbor fence.

The end of the train was crossing the trestle now, and the *Scott* was moving through the deep channel. Cass licked his bleeding palms and hated Ansel Peterson as he watched the ship pass.

It was long and narrow and, now that it was loaded, low in the water. The ship tooted, so loud that Cass felt the boulders quake under him and the ticklish soles of his feet vibrate against his sneakers. Tongue whined as he always did when whistles blew, twitching his ears and shaking his head. The man at the ship's wheel lifted his cap to the people on the shore, and several crewmen leaning on a rail at the back of the cabin waved.

Angry though he was, Cass was amazed as always by the ore boat. It seemed close enough to touch until he saw a crewman leaning on a rail, too far away for Cass to see his face clearly. When someone walked from the bow toward the tall cabin at the stern, checking hatch covers, Cass remembered that the boat was a thousand feet long, longer than three football fields, longer than the city block he used to live on back home.

As he watched the sailors prepare for their voyage across the Great Lakes, Cass seethed. He imagined punching Ansel and knocking him down in front of the football team. Then he thought of Ansel the Great, trying to cover the hole Tongue had made in the seat of his pants, and smiled. Maybe that was revenge enough for now.

The *Scott* tooted a greeting to the waiting *Madge*, then turned and headed out into the lake. Across the water from Cass, on the other side of the buoy that bobbed in the wake of the ship, the last of the sun still lighted the island which lay parallel to the shore, sheltering it and creating this natural harbor. Gulls came and went, squawking and gathering their last meal before dark.

Cass stiffly climbed down the rock face again and limped up behind Eileen. The people from Cabin 1 smiled and waved as they drove away, the gravel crackling under their tires. Mom still stood clinging to the fence, looking out at the wake of the *Scott*.

"Now I can see why you hate Ansel," said Eileen. "He's never acted that way when I was at the Petersons' playing with Liv."

Mom turned, and Cass saw that the chain-link

pattern of the fence had marked her forehead. "How're you doing?" she said to Cass with a gentle touch on his cheek. "Let's go home and build a fire. I'll make you some popcorn."

By the time they reached home, night had fallen. The sign on the highway, CASSIDY CABINS, was brightly lit. The NO VACANCY flap was down, since they had rented the four housekeeping cabins to tourists before dinner.

The Kennedy family had taken over the resort when Mom's parents retired in Arizona, both to keep the land in the family and to supplement Dad's income. Most of their September customers were elderly people who had come back every year when their families were young and Mom was a girl. Now they still returned. When the leaves began to change, they drove northeast along the lakeshore toward the Canadian border to savor the wild burning colors of the autumn woods.

As the Kennedys passed the lighted cabins, Cass saw the foursome from the gray car playing cards at a kitchen table. In Number 2, another couple were just sitting down to eat.

His mother pulled the car up at the side of their own house. "Popcorn!" she said.

"Cider!" said Cass.

"Candy bars and peanut butter sandwiches and sirloin steak and cotton candy!" said Eileen. "There's the *Scott*, way up here already."

Tongue rushed into the trees with his ears pricked, chasing some scent or sound. Cass stood with his mother and sister on the front lawn that sloped down to the rocky bluff, and looked out at Lake Superior. They saw the harvest moon, enormous and golden on the horizon, spilling melted butter across the water to the shore. The *Scott* sailed through the darkness with only its yellow lights visible, like a fairy palace headed for the moon.

"It looks like the maple tree in our old front yard," said Cass, "all lit up for Christmas."

He was bursting with a confusion of feelings. He loved the changing beauty of this freshwater sea, with its unobstructed horizon and sudden weather. Fishing with his mother, he would feel his chin rise into the wind with exultation as the boat thudded into the waves.

Yet he longed for home in Minneapolis. He wondered what the kids were doing down there now. Probably playing Frisbee under the street light while the bats and nighthawks looped and zoomed in the sky overhead.

Mr. Richards would be calling his children from a game of kick-the-can. "Holl-yyyy! Raaa-chel!" he would call, and Rachel would mutter curses under her breath.

Mrs. Peltier would be watering her lawn, not with the sprinkler, but holding the hose in her hand, while David and Eric hunted for fishing worms in the grass.

Cass turned to look at his mother. With shock, he

wondered what she used to feel in Minneapolis when she looked out the kitchen window and her only horizon was the roofline of the garages in the alley.

"Were you as homesick, when we lived back home," he said, "as I am now?" He hugged his mother, and she gathered her children against her warm sweatshirt.

She began to say Saint Patrick's Rune, the blessing she had spoken at bedtime every night for as long as Cass could remember.

"I place all heaven with its power," she said, "and the sun with its brightness, and the snow with its whiteness, and fire with all the strength it hath."

Eileen joined in. "And lightning with its rapid wrath, and the winds with their swiftness along their path."

Cass's husky voice joined the others'. "And the sea with its deepness, and the rocks with their steepness, and the earth with its starkness: all these I place, by God's almighty help and grace, between ourselves and the powers of darkness."

Thinking with dread about going to school and facing Ansel on Monday, Cass began to shiver.

"Oh, Cass," said Mom. "Yes — I was homesick then. And I'm homesick now."

Two

Cass's bedroom faced the sunrise. As soon as day began to break, Tongue cold-nosed his neck, and Cass jumped out of bed. He never wasted a moment of Saturday if he could help it.

He found a flannel shirt under his bed, entangled in a short but noisy length of rusty chain Mom had found near Two Harbors, washed ashore in a storm at the place where the *Lafayette* went aground in 1905. He laid the souvenir carefully down on a dirty sock to keep it quiet.

Since his parents delayed starting the furnace as late in the year as possible, trying not to waste fuel, Cass's room was cold. He shivered as he buttoned his shirt, starting at the bottom as Mom had taught him one morning back home after he buttoned up crooked three times running. Tongue sat back, smiling and cocking his head and sweeping the varnished floor with his heavy tail.

The dog shoved ahead on the stairs. "Why do you always have to be first in line?" Cass said.

He stuffed a bag of granola into his pocket, grabbed his piece of rope, and shut the screen door quietly behind him. A swallow dashed out of the mud nest that had been plastered under the eaves near the door since spring. In August, it had been full of gaping mouths, babies squeaking their need from dawn to dusk. They were gone now.

"Go back to sleep," said Cass to the swallow. "The bugs aren't up yet."

As he passed his father's state police car, parked between the old family clunker and the snowmobile, covered with its khaki tarp, Cass stopped to write his name in the frost on the maroon hood. He had fallen asleep last night before Dad came home from his evening shift. He wished for the thousandth time that his father still taught school or at least worked regular days like other people. If he worked in the woods cutting timber like some of the other kids' fathers, he could be home at suppertime every night.

Under his name on the car hood, Cass drew an unhappy face, a circle with two dots for eyes and an inverted smile. Then he ran after Tongue, who had already rushed across the frosty yard past the cabins and picked his way down the face of the twenty-foot cliff. Mounds and billows and sheets of rock poured from the cliff down into the water, spilled there by a volcano that had guttered out and disappeared hundreds of millions of years ago. Often the waves crashed halfway up the side of the cliff, but today the water just licked the rocks at the bottom. Across the lake, the sun was a finger's width above the horizon, staining the water and sky pink and lavender and pale, faint green.

Down the shore from the Kennedy place, where the land was low and a pebble beach stretched between the water and the high ground above, Cass saw a huge bird.

"Heel," he said to Tongue. Looking downtrodden, with his ears and tail drooped, the dog came to Cass and sat down beside his left leg. "You'd chase that bird away, and I want a good look at him."

The bird was gray, with rust-colored wings, a skinny neck, and a long, pointed beak. It stood three or four feet tall, on long legs that looked too flimsy to support its heavy body. It faced across the water, as if it had merely stopped in the midst of its errands to enjoy the sunrise.

Cass held Tongue's collar and watched the bird for a long time. When it didn't move, Cass inched closer. The bird took a few awkward steps toward the water, thrusting its head forward as it walked. Tongue saw it or caught its scent. Unable to contain himself, he broke loose and rushed ahead.

"Here, Tongue! Stop! Sit! Stay!" yelled Cass.

The dog paused, looking confused, but he stopped too late. The bird began to run clumsily and then lifted itself on its huge rusty wings and flapped away down the shore.

"Darn you, Tongue," said Cass. "You've got no sense. I'll probably never see that bird again."

Far down the curving shore, at the mouth of the river, Cass saw Mun Benson already at work on his fishing nets. At that distance the old man was little more than a dot.

Munson Benson and Cassidy Kennedy, Cass thought, smiling once again at the singularity of their rhyming names. Munson and Cassidy had been their mothers' family names. That coincidence had brought them together, but Cass had found that he had more than odd facts in common with the old man.

He set off down the beach, trudging across stones that pulled at his feet as Tongue ran rapidly ahead.

Halfway to Mr. Benson's place, Cass climbed the rising ground to the top of the high cliffs. Here, even on a calm day, deep, green water slapped the rock, curled back upon itself, and rushed away in eddies and whirlpools and foam.

This was the place mapmakers had romantically named Indian Deep, but which the fishermen, knowing its history more intimately, called the boat-butcher. Cass resisted the temptation to check the cave he had found last summer. He would stop there on his way home, as he did every Saturday.

By the time Cass reached Benson's place a mile downshore from home, the sun was well up. Tongue had already exchanged greetings with the old man, had had his head patted and his ears scratched, and had disappeared into the woods, where there were always fresh deer tracks leading down to the river.

Tongue never joined the dog pack that ran deer to exhaustion; he was too old and too attached to Cass and too citified to go off with a mob of half-wild dogs. But he was always curious about the tracks and droppings of animals.

The boy and the old man nodded at each other.

"I've got my knot you showed me down pat," said Cass.

With the piece of rope he carried in his pocket, he demonstrated on an upright post where the nets were wound on a huge wooden reel.

"What do you call this knot?" Cass asked.

"I know how to do it, but I never bothered with the name for it."

Cass could hear the lilting Danish accent that Mun Benson had never lost, even though he had left Denmark as a young man and had never gone back. "That's pretty good," Mr. Benson said. "Can you tie it with your eyes closed?"

Cass tried, but the rope fell at his feet.

"If you come up to your buoy or a dock in the dark, you've got to be able to tie up as easy as you breathe," said Mr. Benson. "Fishermen know their knots without looking."

As they talked, the old man worked a shuttle quickly in and out, bridging a hole in the big net with a loose latticework of knots, while Cass practiced a different knot on the post.

Tongue trotted back into the clearing now and

visited each of Mr. Benson's buildings. Below them on the beach was the fish house where he cleaned and packed his catch. The cabin, old and faded enough to look like a natural growth, stood at the edge of the woods. The delicious aroma of smoke and cooking fish seeped through cracks and around the door of the smallest building, where the fisherman smoked herring and trout for sale.

In the cliff at the side of the yard was the cave with precisely fitted doors, where Mun Benson stored supplies and large tools. When Cass had found the other cave up the shore, he kept it a secret, hoping to fit it out as a usable shelter like Mr. Benson's.

"Look at the mist," said Cass. Even though the sky was blue and the sun brilliant on the water, wisps and clouds of fog shifted along the shoreline, sometimes thick enough to blur the trees.

"It was a clear morning like this twenty-five years ago when the lake almost got me."

Cass perked up his ears. He had never heard the same story twice from this old man, who had a thousand stories to tell but little need for an admiring audience. He told stories as one might report a scene in a telescope, as if he were watching the events of his youth unfold. In fact, the high school history teacher so admired his clear memory for details that she invited him to speak every year about North Shore history.

Mr. Benson shivered and buttoned his threadbare

lumberjack coat close at his throat. He pulled his cap down on his forehead, as if to fix it there against a wind.

"This is the boat, here."

He reached under the big overturned boat that he and Cass had been scraping for weeks, preparing it for new paint, and brought out a wire brush and a steel scraper. Cass took the brush and began to work on the patches Mr. Benson had already scraped.

The fisherman was a leisurely storyteller who couldn't be hurried. "Never trust the weather on Superior," he said. "Treacherous as a wildcat. Look away, blink your eyes, and she pounces. Many's the ship that's smashed to smithereens on those rocks between here and your place."

Mr. Benson scraped and Cass brushed.

"The air was clear as I ever saw it that day when I started out. The lake was as flat as water on a plate. Along about noon, fog began to roll in. In fifteen minutes, the shoreline was gone. Before long, a gale was blowing so hard I couldn't tell which was rain and which was lake."

"You had your engine, didn't you?"

"You can't trust these damn fool machines any more than you can trust the lake. I'd just started back when she give out."

"Didn't you have oars?"

"This ain't a rowboat, Cass, and that ain't a mill-pond."

The old man rubbed the white stubble on his jaw,

his pale blue eyes staring into the distance. "But those was the days before the lamprey eel killed off the lake trout. There was fishermen all up and down the shore, and the fishermen keep together. When I don't come home, my wife, she told the other men."

Cass heard Mr. Benson's accent thicken and his grammar become careless.

"In the night, the rain turned to sleet, and the temperature fell. This boat can wade through deep waves. See how high the gunwales are and how wide she is at the waist? That's why I still scrape her and paint her and keep her in shape, even though the other boat's newer." He pointed at the steel fishing boat tied to a buoy offshore.

Cass watched Mr. Benson smooth away the loose paint and stray fish scales with his hand as gently as a boy pets a dog. He tried not to look at the stumps of the old man's missing fingers.

"See these boards here?" Mr. Benson pointed at the bow of the boat. "I splintered the wood that night and had to replace these boards. The boat stay afloat if she don't swamp. I don't even try to get home, but only to stay afloat. Most of the night, I lie in the bottom of the boat, out of the wind, covered with a tarp. But every little while I have to break the ice off the gunwales with the hatchet I keep in the tool box in the stern. The ice built up and made her heavy."

He held up his mutilated right hand. No matter how many times Cass saw it, he still felt his stomach flip. The two end fingers were gone entirely, and the tip of the forefinger.

"Froze 'em."

Cass looked away and changed the subject. "How could they find you on this — ocean?"

"The Coast Guard was out, but it was the fishermen who knew where I set my nets, which way the wind blowed, what the lake was bound to do to a boat like mine. They know the lake the way Tongue knows the woods around your place. These are people who can go out five mile in a fog so deep you can't see your own hand and stop right on the buoy that marks their nets. Found me the next day ten mile out, away down by the Cutthroat River."

Cass shivered, uneasily thinking of the danger in the lake which looked so placid now. He wondered what capsized sailors felt when they found themselves doomed in that frigid water.

"I tried swimming in the lake one hot day this summer," Cass said, trying to think of more pleasant things. "But the cold water made me ache so much I couldn't stand it more than two or three minutes at a time."

"You fall out of your boat in the spring, you don't last ten minutes," Mr. Benson said. "We have a saying: Superior never gives up her dead. You sink to the bottom in this cold water, and the bottom's a long way down."

The old man gazed at the shimmering surface of the water. "The Indians talked about the tall water here. They meant deep. She's a thousand feet deep, the biggest lake in the world. Enough water to drown all of New England. Swim in the river pools, Cass. There's a pool up there where the water's so deep you can dive off a ten-foot cliff."

"Yeah. My mother drove us up there once in a while last summer. After we finished cleaning the cabins, she just dropped the No Vacancy flap for an hour and swam with us," said Cass. "She used to swim in that deep pool above the gorge when she was a girl."

He thought of how unfamiliar to him his own life had become. "Back home in Minneapolis, my dad and I used to swim at Lake Harriet every night after supper," he said. "But now he says he doesn't have time."

"You and me, we both left home and come to a foreign country, didn't we?" said Mr. Benson. "My father, now, he was a fancy Copenhagen lawyer. I wanted adventure, but when I come here, I think I can't live without the wine and crystal chandeliers. What I think is adventure turns out to be mostly hard work."

They worked in companionable silence for a while.

"Did you see the crane?" Mr. Benson asked.

"The one down at the harbor?"

Mr. Benson laughed. "Not the machine. The bird. There's a big sandhill crane hanging around here. Walks on stilts. Near as tall as you are."

"He was on the beach this morning," said Cass. "The one with the rust-colored wings?"

Mr. Benson nodded. "He's been nesting in some marsh inland where the iron colors the water red. That's what stained his feathers. He pokes his beak into the mud looking for food and then strokes his wings," said Mr. Benson. "Sandhills used to be scarce, but they're coming back. Never saw one on the beach, though."

"Before we moved, I was planning to study birds at the Science Museum back home."

"Oh, ya. I know. When I was a boy, we had the big museums in Copenhagen too." Benson waved his arm in a gesture that encompassed the woods and the sky and the lake. "This here museum will keep you busy learning all your life. Then you die, just beginning to understand what's here."

Cass thought of a line from *Moby Dick* that his mother liked to say — "The sea was my Harvard and my Yale."

"Do you suppose any of your friends in Minneapolis bumped into a sandhill crane on the beach at Lake Harriet today?" Mr. Benson asked.

"Tongue scared the bird away this morning," said Cass, avoiding Mr. Benson's irony, but smiling at the thought of the shy crane walking with a police escort among the crowds of skaters, joggers, cyclists, and sunbathers at the city lake. Those who didn't chase it would flee from it in fear.

"Where'd that dog get to?" said Cass, looking

around. "I have to clean the cabins when the tourists leave."

He whistled with his thumb and forefinger in his mouth, a skill Dad had taught him the summer before they moved north, when life was never too busy for fun. The loud, piercing note still surprised and pleased Cass every time.

Tongue ran out of the woods. "Time for breakfast, old boy," said Cass. "We'll see you next Saturday, Mr. Benson."

"Ya. Practice your knots in the dark."

Three

On the way down to Mun Benson's place, Cass had walked as near the water as he could, climbing the bluff only where the waves lapped the cliff near his own cave and forced him up to higher ground. Going home, he chose the high ground all the way, planning to skirt the pond that lay in a cedar swamp between the road and the lake. Maybe he would see the moose that had stayed there all summer.

The swamp was not wet at this time of year, after a long dry summer, although springs kept the pond filled the year round. There was moss on everything, like a plush carpet that conformed to every surface and softened every angle. The ground was so springy under the hummocks of grass and the network of moss-covered sticks that Cass thought water must underlie the vegetation. But now, in the autumn, his shoes stayed dry.

Cass sat down on a log cushioned with moss and unwrapped the bag of granola he had carried in his jeans pocket. The smell of the cedar swamp always took him back to his baby days, when he had loved looking at the baby books, the faded wedding bouquet, and other treasures his mother stored in a deep cedar chest.

Whenever Mom opened that old chest, a wild atmosphere had risen out of the pink wood and filled the room. The same piney smell permeated this cedar swamp, especially in the morning and the evening, when the dew was heavy and the air damp.

The trees themselves were gracefully twisted, with a shaggy, silky gray bark and thick evergreen foliage. Cass reached back and picked a cedar twig to replace the old one he had carried in his pocket for a week. He could transport himself out of school whenever he chose, or off the schoolbus or away from the dishpan, by crushing the twig between his fingers, smelling its wild odor and imagining himself far away in the cedar thicket, where the light was green and ghostly. He thought that Saint Patrick should have added a line to his blessing about the swamps with their strangeness.

As he sat thinking, Cass nibbled the granola, which was still warm from his pocket. He listened to the whining sound of cars and semi trucks passing on the road up near the Petersons' place, and watched scores of ants madly racing hither and thither on the log where he was sitting, on the mossy ground by his feet, and even on his legs.

Something stung his thigh, then the calf of his other leg, then both calves and his ankle and knee—

cap and the back of his knee. He jumped to his feet and tried to unbutton his jeans, but he had grown during the summer, and they were tight at the waist. He slapped his legs and struggled to get the copper button through the buttonhole, slapped his legs some more and fought with the zipper.

He stripped off his pants and brushed at the troops of ants that were running up and down his legs, biting as they went. Mistaking his frantic dance and yelps of pain for play, Tongue jumped up on Cass's shoulders and knocked him down. As he thrashed around, trying to fend off Tongue so he could give the ants all the attention they deserved, he accidentally punched the dog in the nose. Tongue yipped in injured surprise and crawled under a fallen tree, leaving Cass to his misery.

When he had scattered all the ants, Cass assessed the damage on the battleground: bites on top of welts overlapping bites. He turned his pants inside out and brushed them thoroughly before he put them back on.

"Sorry, old Tongue," he told the dog, trying to coax him out of the lair where he was moping. "Now I know what Mom means when I'm so restless she says I've got ants in my pants."

Before long, the dog regained his high spirits. He had been larking ahead most of the way all morning, with his rabies tag and name tag jingling on his collar. But as they approached the pond, Cass called him with a hand signal. He was amazed when Tongue obeyed. Holding the collar with the tags quieted in his hand, Cass walked as stealthily as he could through the bushes that grew thick at the edge of the pond. Alders, Dad had said.

Hearing a stick crack somewhere across the pond, Cass and Tongue froze. There, grazing in the water, was the young cow moose that Cass had hoped to see. She stood knee-deep in the pond, chewing long-stemmed aquatic plants that hung down like a beard from her mouth. The sunlight dappled her brown hide.

As Cass and the moose looked each other in the eye, Tongue smelled her. He broke loose, splashed into the water, and began to swim across the pond, as enthusiastic as if he had a chance of catching the moose. At the first splash, she plunged out of the water and trotted away. Her long legs looked as gangly and ill-matched to her body as the crane's, but, far from being clumsy, she was fast enough to be dangerous to humans.

"Come here, dummy," yelled Cass. "You're a re-triever, but she's not a duck. She's half a mile away by now."

Tongue gave up in the middle of the pond. He swam back to shore, slogged through the shallow, muddy water at the edge, and reported for duty at Cass's feet, looking out of the corner of his eye at the boy. Then he shimmied and shook himself, trans-ferring the water off his waterproof coat and onto Cass.

Before he could protect himself, Cass got a face full of mud. The front side of his legs were wet, and his purple football jacket was speckled with black spots.

"Sabotage," he said, wiping his face on his sleeve. "I'm never ready for you, am I?"

Headed toward home again, they cut back through the cedar woods. They went through a stand of birches, and then among closely growing hardwoods, oaks and maples that must have been too small when the loggers had scalped the land decades ago. They came out just where Cass had planned, at the place by the forked spruce where an old overgrown logging road met the lake. He was pleased that his sense of direction was so sure.

I know these woods like the kids in Minneapolis know their backyards, he thought, still smarting a bit from Mr. Benson's remarks about museums. And it hasn't taken me a lifetime either. He imagined that he could survive alone, by now, with no equipment except his knife. Could Ansel the Great do that, he wondered? Ansel didn't even know he had a moose living next door to him in the swamp.

Cass and Tongue followed the cliff about two hundred yards toward home. Back among the rocks near the edge of the woods was the cave Cass had found, a broad split in the rock, four or five feet wide at the bottom, and six or eight feet deep, with a low ceiling of rock and tree roots. Such caves were fairly common here, in a landscape littered with boulders and cliffs that looked like a giant baby's building blocks. Cass crouched to enter the cave, where he had been stashing equipment and supplies all summer.

He was glad that he had told no one about this secret place, not Mr. Benson, not Eileen, not even Mom. It was the only place he had ever had to himself. I'm practically in Ansel's backyard, he thought smugly, but the great woodsman hasn't even noticed.

He looked around the cave, surveying its contents. There was the hatchet, the blade covered with Vaseline to prevent rusting, and several candle stubs stored inside an instant-coffee jar. He had filled a horseradish bottle with wooden matches and sealed the lid by dipping it in paraffin to keep them dry. The head of each match he had also sealed with wax, which would scrape off when he struck it on rock. In a tin cookie box, protected from dampness and the mice that would have chewed up the paper for nests, were Cass's Boy Scout manual and his favorite book of Irish fairy tales.

If Dad had known about the cave, Cass thought, he would have spoiled the fun with a joke. "What are you doing," he imagined Dad saying, "stocking up for a week-long air raid?" So Cass had taken old things that wouldn't be missed, or his own equipment, or food that he bought himself.

In a large, tight potato chip can, protected from chipmunks and squirrels, he had stuffed an old pair of pants, a suit of long underwear, and a shirt, in case he fell in the pond in cold weather or some disaster marooned him here.

Where the cave narrowed to a point at the back, he had stacked dry logs and kindling, enough wood to keep a fire going, he figured, for a couple of days. He sometimes imagined himself running away — he would lie low here and then hitchhike to Minneapolis to see his friends. Someday his foresight and planning might even save his family during a war.

He had spent most of his summer's allowance on food. On top of the change of clothes was a bag of dried apple slices, a box of raisins, a jumbo chocolate bar, and a can of shoestring potatoes. Stacked on the ground beside the food can were several small containers of orange juice, a can of root beer, a jar of dried beef, and one can each of Vienna sausages and alphabet soup.

Checking his stores, Cass thought that some of the food was missing. He had suspected before that candy and other supplies had disappeared, but he had never been certain. He ate the inventory and replaced it so fast, he couldn't remember for sure.

His stomach growled as he crawled out of the cave. He opened the bag of apple slices and the can of root beer and sat down to eat another breakfast under the solitary Norway pine that had found a foothold decades ago in a crack in the rocks, halfway between the cave and the edge of the cliff.

Far out on the glimmering lake, an ore boat was

almost out of sight, dropping below the horizon, trailing a plume of smoke behind it. South of the ship, a long, low black cloud glowered, draining its dark contents into the lake. Although the sky was clear overhead, Cass could see lightning flash in the distance, miles out on the lake.

Above him, a few gulls dropped by, tilting on the wind, their wings translucent in the sunlight. They were looking for an invitation to breakfast. When none was offered, two of them alighted above Cass in the pine and watched his every bite.

Today, although he wouldn't like to admit it, Cass felt at home here on the shore, and the city seemed like a dream. He only wished that David, who had lived in the house across the alley, could be here too.

"Apples and root beer sure taste funny together," he said aloud.

Tongue stared at the apple chips. Then he stared at Cass and drooled until the boy gave in. He flipped slices of fruit into the air like coins, and the dog caught them on the way down with a loud chomp.

"Who ever heard of a dog that liked apples?" said Cass. "But then, who ever heard of a dog that liked tomatoes, either?" His family joked every year about planting a private patch for Tongue, who wouldn't leave the young tomatoes alone, but gobbled as many as he could reach through the fence when they were still green.

When his breakfast was all gone, Cass gathered a handful of pebbles. Lying on his belly, he dropped them one by one over the edge of the cliff, watching them fall between stunted trees, fifty feet to the deep water below. The long drop always made him queasy.

He noticed then how high the sun stood in the sky. Thinking of his chores, he reluctantly stood up and stretched. "I'm supposed to be cleaning cabins and washing sheets!" he told the dog.

He threw his last rock as far out into the lake as he could, watched for the splash, and then headed for home. He ran all the way. Maybe he could sneak in and get the work done before Dad caught up with him.

Four

When Cass ambled into the yard, breathless with hurrying but trying to look casual, his father was mowing the broad front lawn on the tractor. He shifted the engine to idle and jumped down.

"Afternoon, son." He looked at his watch. "Ten o'clock already. The cabins were vacated an hour ago."

"I went down to Mr. Benson's."

"Since you weren't here to share the job with Eileen, I told her you'd do it alone. She went to see Liv."

Cass saw Tongue skulk away and crawl under a cabin to hide. "Dad, I tried to be back by nine, but I got held up."

"Oh, yes?"

"I saw a sandhill crane down on the beach."

"That's an interesting thing to see, all right."

"And that moose was up by the cedar swamp again."

"A thing like that'll keep a boy away from work all day."

"Yeah, and the moose charged, and Tongue went after him to protect me."

Cass knew that his story was unlikely, and he could see that his father was smiling maliciously, letting him get deeper into his lie. But he couldn't stop himself.

"I barely got away. . . ."

The sudden storm on his father's face, the fading smile, and the dark eyes piercing Cass's own silenced the boy.

"No more drama, Cass! You're not a little boy anymore, making up innocent stories."

Cass felt humiliated. "You don't believe me, do you? Why don't you ever believe me?"

"Why do you think I don't believe you?"

"Can I get started on the cabins?"

"No. We've got business, Cass. If you make a mistake don't make excuses. You went down the beach, and you got back late. Fine. You lost track of time. But *you* messed up, not some trumped-up moose."

"But Dad, you don't understand," Cass pleaded, desperate to justify himself in his father's eyes.

"This is not an argument, Cass."

"Whatever you say," said Cass, an edge of defiance in his voice.

"Cut it, Cass!" Usually so calm and gentle, Dad was suddenly shouting and squeezing Cass's shoulder in a bruising grip. "Have you any idea what it's

36

been like for me, to go from teaching the brightest students at Central to arresting drunk tourists on the back roads of Minnesota?"

Cass was shocked by the tears in the corners of his father's eyes. "You're hurting me, Dad," he said, trying to pull away.

Dad released him and looked with a puzzled expression at his own hand. "Everybody up here is Mom's old childhood friend, and I don't know a blessed soul."

"You expect *me* to come up here and fit right in, though!" Cass said, infuriated.

"Here I am," said Dad, deaf to Cass's anger, "a city Irishman in a country of Swedes. We have to drive forty minutes to get to Mass."

"You expect *me* to do it without blinking!" shouted Cass. "You never asked me how I felt about moving!" His father seemed not to hear.

"Why'd you have to bring me up here to the sticks?" Cass said more softly, noticing the gray that had grown in Dad's black sideburns during the past year. "We never do anything together anymore, Dad. You're always working around here when you're not on patrol."

"Is that what makes you so sore?"

"You gave me that big chemistry set, but we've only played with it twice. Every time I wanted you to go swimming with me, you had to split wood." Cass wailed with the pain of what he was saying. "I'm lonesome, Dad."

Dad looked him in the face, refusing to bend. "What you could do when you're lonesome is help with the work. I'm stretched to the limit trying to fix up all the things Grandpa let go before he retired. Help me split that wood, Cass."

Cass turned away, angry. "That's not what I mean. All you can think of is work."

"We might go down to the Cities and stay with Grandma Kennedy for a few days during Christmas vacation," said Dad. Cass's spirits brightened.

"Right now, though, we've got our problems here to deal with." Dad leaned back against the tractor. "I hear you've been telling a lot of big ones, Cass. You and I are going to hunt bear with pistols? You and I were a detective team back home?"

"I never said we were detectives. I suppose Eileen told you that."

"No. The men were laughing about you down at Petersons' last night."

Cass groaned. The back side of Petersons' house, next to the highway, was a small grocery store and bar where people from miles around got together evenings to talk and enjoy the company of friends. Cass avoided the place in order to avoid Ansel.

"How'd they find out?"

"Their kids told them."

"Those hotshot kids brag so much about hunting, they couldn't tell the difference between lies and truth," Cass sputtered. "All they care about is killing things. If I told them about my moose, they'd shoot her."

"It's hard to explain to our friends up here why you and I don't enjoy hunting, Cass." He gave his son a searching look. "But we don't have to lie about who we are to be worthwhile people. And we don't have to hate them for being different from us."

Cass wanted to throw his arms around his father, to be swung up on the man's tall shoulders, to be carried home on high and ducked through the door. But he held himself back and stared across the lake with his jaws clenched.

"A diller, a dollar, a ten o'clock scholar." The words of the nursery rhyme, one of the beloved formulas of warm and cozy days, flashed through his head, and he muttered them, as if to call those old days back.

"What's that?" said Dad.

"Nothing," said Cass, feeling stubborn. "Never mind."

Dad had said Cass wasn't a little boy anymore, and only little boys say nursery rhymes, Cass thought. No one, not even Mom, and certainly not Dad, could understand how sad he felt.

"Cass, I'm glad you can forget everything but the lake and the woods. I never saw a sandhill crane in my life." Dad's voice sounded wistful. "You may not feel at home quite yet, but you're making a place for yourself here." He patted Cass's shoulder. "But do your work, and try to get along at school. And don't lie to me."

Dad climbed back on the tractor, and Cass headed for Cabin 1, to clean it before the next batch of travelers arrived. He was disappointed that Dad had not read his mind or made him explain his sadness.

"It's safe to come out now, Tongue." The dog crept sheepishly from under a cabin, a spiderweb across his black nose. "Coward," said Cass. "You left me in the lurch again."

He smelled the bleach and the cleanser as the screen door of Cabin 1 slammed shut. In the kitchen, Eileen was rinsing the sink. She had already cleaned the stove and propped open the refrigerator door.

"Dad said I had to clean the cabins alone," said Cass. "He said you went to see Liv."

"I'll do that later. Just now I cut through the woods and climbed the cliffs in the front of the cabins. Dad didn't see me," Eileen said. "I'm sorry I was mean in the car last night."

"It doesn't matter," said Cass. "Thanks for helping out. I thought I'd be doing cabins till sundown."

Cleaning up after these tourists was easy. Sometimes hunters left everything dirty, even the frying pans. Others washed the frying pans, but stole the toaster. Once Cass's grandmother had found a quarter-pound of butter stuck to the bedroom ceiling.

The old people who came to see the autumn leaves, however, left the cabins as tidy as they found them, with the shower and bathroom sink washed and dried, the floor swept, and every chair tucked neatly under the red plaid oilcloth on the table.

Cass pulled a sagging double bed away from the wall. The sheets and blankets were folded precisely at the foot of the bed, the heater turned off, and the window opened a crack to air the room.

"Mom ought to leave clean bed linen in the cabins when these people come," he said. "I bet they'd even make up the beds for us."

He looked out the front window and watched the waves breaking over the rocks below. This cabin, built by Grandpa Cassidy with huge pine logs, sat right on the edge of the cliff. The head of the bed was as close to the water as it could be.

Sometimes when business was slow, Mom let Cass sleep here, listening to the water swish or crash over the rocks, depending on the weather. "Just so you clean up the cabin when you're done," she always said. Cass loved to watch the storms, when the lightning flashed like fireworks over the lake.

"Dad says that in a couple of weeks, he'll shut off the water and close the cabins for the winter," said Eileen. "Then we won't have to do any work on Saturday mornings."

"Don't worry, they'll think of something," Cass said. "They think work is good for kids. Besides, it'll be so cold by then, we won't care if we have free time."

"You could learn how to ski, you know."

Cass punched a pillow until dust and feathers

made him sneeze. "Are you going to start that again? I don't want to ski. I don't want to be like Ansel Peterson." His voice dripped acid.

"I just wish you had more fun here."

"I have fun. I've got a moose down the lake, and a sandhill crane, and a few other things that are secret."

As sudden rain clattered on the cabin roof, Cass sprawled across the clean bed. He leaned his forehead against the bars of the iron bedstead and stared out the window. South across the lake, far beyond the gray horizon, was David, the Science Museum, the sweet old days, home.

Five

As autumn continued its long slide down into winter, Cass watched the woods change. The birches and quaking aspen had turned yellow in September, and the sumac in the ditches changed to red. Then the maples flared up like supernovas, brilliant yellow, orange and pink against the dark green spruces. Oak leaves glowed red as poured wine until they gradually dried and turned brittle and brown, sticking on the trees after the other leaves fell.

From the schoolbus, Cass saw the woods change a little every day, and watched the ice build up along the shore. The spray froze on the rocks and cliffs every night in icicles or lacy fretwork or rounded hulks that in the dawn light reminded Cass of dinosaurs. He often saw ships steaming far offshore, hurrying to get in a few last trips before the lake froze up.

When Cass and Eileen boarded the bus one morning in mid-October, she rushed ahead, as she usually did, and flopped into the seat beside Liv, as she always did. Cass nodded at Mrs. Larson, the bus driver.

"Here's the great hunter from Minneapolis," said Ansel, who reserved the front seat for himself and whichever friend was his current favorite. Ben Brewer sat there today.

Ansel's sneer was a cue for the other boys. "Yeah, I suppose you and your dad are going to hunt bear with squirt guns and pea shooters," said Ben.

"He and his dad are going to sprinkle salt on timber wolves' tails," said Todd Andersen, known as Toad by his friends.

Cass looked straight ahead down the aisle, as if the bus were empty. Cheerleader, he thought, feeling his hate for Ansel rise in his throat. Jeerleader.

"Look at him! He's going to cry!" said Ansel. "Did your mama pin your diapers too tight?"

Eileen threw a piece of candy among the boys, who lost interest in Cass as they scrambled for it. Skellying, the kids called that ploy, but it reminded Cass of the story of Cadmus, who, attacked by warriors, threw a rock in their midst and set them to fighting among themselves.

The bus lurched forward before Cass had reached his regular seat. At the same time, Todd stuck out his foot. Cass tripped and stumbled, trying to regain his balance, all the way to the back of the bus. He fell into his seat beside Magda.

Nobody else would sit there, and nobody except Eileen would let Cass sit anywhere else. Magda Potter was a first-grader, with a big family of older and younger children. She always chose the seat over the heater, and she always smelled of urine. She was asleep, as usual, with her head shucked down inside the collar of her raggedy jacket.

Cass had made a mask of his face to hide his rage and sadness. His eyes were swollen with tears he hadn't allowed to form. He stared out the window until the bus passed the hill where he had once seen a bear looking out from the thick brush. Then he opened his notebook and finished his long-division problems.

Cass always did his homework on the bus. The teachers complained about his sloppy handwriting, but they complained about that no matter how hard he tried. While Eileen labored at the kitchen table after the evening dishes were done, Cass practiced his knots or read his books about survival. Or he watched ore boats on the lake and looked at the stars through the big telescope Mom and Dad had bought him for Christmas and set up by the picture window. Eileen made better grades in school, but Cass knew more about the stars.

When his math was done, Cass shut his notebook and watched the roadside. His powers of observation were growing, like the alertness of a good detective. Now he could distinguish between a hawk and an eagle in flight. He often saw deer that he thought nobody else noticed.

Every day he watched for a fox that had a den on a hillside among some half-grown jackpines. He had found her at home several times, sitting like a dog on a mound of earth at the entrance of her den, watching the road. He never got more than a glimpse, but a glimpse was enough to make the ride fun. Cass felt smug about the other boys, who heckled each other and put pine cones down the girls' necks, missing the things he saw.

When they were nearing the school, the bus and Dad's police car passed each other on the road. Dad was working the day shift that month. Each driver tooted a greeting. Cass waved, excited, trying to get his dad's attention.

The boys on the bus began to chant: "Cops are pigs! Cops are pigs! Cops are pigs!"

Then the oinking started. Ansel Peterson had turned around, grinning at Cass and grunting like a pig. All the boys joined him — a herd of pigs oinking and snorting and pushing their noses up.

Cass tried to ignore Ansel and the others. He knew that everybody along the shore liked Dad, who didn't give many speeding tickets, but spent most of his time helping out neighbors — people like old Mrs. Hart, who ran out of heating oil in the dead of February last year, or the driver of this bus, Kay Larson, whose car had stalled during the worst blizzard of the winter. The kids liked Dad, too. They only wanted to get Cass's goat.

He tried to hide his fury the way Eileen was doing. She laughed and yelled, "Wait till we get to school. They slop the hogs in the lunchroom at noon."

But the insult to his father was an insult to Cass. It was too much. "Stop it!" he yelled. "Shut your creepy mouths, you clucks!"

He ran up the aisle, flailing his fists. He punched an Erickson twin in the mouth before the boy could duck. He shoved Ben Brewer almost out of his seat.

With his fists flying, Cass reached across Ben and pummeled Ansel, who covered his face with his forearms and shucked down on the floor, trying to protect himself against the onslaught. Cass was breathing hard and fending off Ben's blows when the bus swerved off the road at a Scenic Rest Area and stopped so suddenly that Cass sprawled across Ben and fell into Ansel's seat. With shock, Cass saw the wad of Ansel's blond hair that he held in his hand.

Mrs. Larson pulled the three boys apart. Pinching the back of his neck in her hand, she propelled Cass back to his seat. He dropped Ansel's tuft of hair as secretly as he could on the floor, but Mrs. Larson saw it fall. She picked up the hair and put it in her pocket.

"All of you boys are on report," she said, turning in the direction of Ansel and Ben. Her fair skin was blotchy with anger. "Warnings go to your parents. One more offense and you'll be kicked off the bus."

She leaned over Cass and asked in a low voice, "What's that terrible smell?"

"Magda wets the bed," Cass whispered. He glanced at Magda, who was snoring.

"We'll send a note about that to her folks, too." Mrs. Larson rested her hand on Cass's shoulder for a moment. "Find a better way to deal with insults, Cass. There are too many bullies in the world to scalp them all."

Six

When Cass and Eileen came in from school a few days later, Tongue was waiting in his usual place at the door. He whined and smiled and pranced at their feet, as if he had thought they were never coming back. Cass ignored him, feeling the tension between Mom and Dad, who sat by the kitchen window warming their hands on cups of hot cider. A letter lay on the table between them.

"What's this letter from Mrs. Larson?" asked Dad, tapping it with his forefinger.

Eileen hesitated momentarily. Then she swung her backpack full of books off one shoulder as she rushed through the kitchen and up the stairs to her room, with Tongue pounding past her.

"Letter?" Refusing to meet Dad's eyes, Cass looked out at the gray lake.

" 'Involved in a fight on the schoolbus,' " Dad read aloud. " 'Probation. Bus privileges suspended in the event of another such incident.' " His voice grew louder with every phrase.

Mom gently touched Dad's hand. "Let's hear what Cass has to say."

"I hate that Ansel Peterson!" Cass said. "You saw him push me off that rock at the harbor, Mom. He does something mean like that every day."

"What happened Tuesday?" asked Mom softly.

"He shoved me against my coat hook last week." Cass fingered the strap on his backpack. He felt desperate to explain that the fight had been building for a long time. "He's always tripping me when I get on the bus. He hits me all the time when nobody's looking."

"How about Tuesday?" asked Dad.

"Here, Cass," said his mother, pouring cider for him into her cup and offering her own chair. "Sit down." He put his loaded backpack on the floor and sat with his parka still fastened tight at the chin.

"Get it over with, Cass," Dad said.

"Ansel insulted me," said Cass unwillingly, embarrassed to admit what had triggered his explosion.

Boards creaked in the bedroom hall. "Ansel Peterson stinks," Eileen called down the stairs. "He called you a pig, Dad."

"Eileen and I have to let out the hem on her skirt," said Mom. She went upstairs, where Cass could hear her talking quietly with Eileen. Cass felt abandoned.

"Why didn't you tell me what's been going on with Ansel?" asked Dad, hitting the table with the flat of his hand. "If you're so secretive, I can't help you."

"Fat lot of help you'd be!" said Cass. "All you ever do is lecture me. 'Grow up, Cass. Keep your nose clean, Cass. Work it out yourself, Cass. Stay out of trouble.' " He glared at his father, who glared back until Cass looked away.

"That's all good advice." Dad paused. "But if you *have* to fight, fight to win." Cass stared out the window through a long silence. "I hear you won this one," Dad said.

Hearing quiet approval in his father's voice, Cass glanced up, surprised. "I guess I did."

"Good," said Dad, getting up from the table and putting his cup in the sink. "I never could stomach bullies, either."

Cass huddled at the table while Dad put on his jacket and went outdoors. Then, feeling dismissed and uneasy, as if something remained unsettled, Cass took his books upstairs to his room. He looked out at the lake, thinking about the lecture and shouting match he had primed himself for and wondering why it hadn't happened.

After a while, Dad came into view, angrily kicking rocks at the edge of the cliff. Cass watched him pick up a pebble and throw it out over the water as hard as he could. Then he thrust his hands into his pants pockets and stood for a long time with his shoulders hunched against the wind, looking south toward home, as Cass himself so often did.

Cass couldn't remember ever seeing Dad stand idle outdoors since they came north. He looked so small against the backdrop of the lake that Cass felt unfamiliar sympathy for him. He was about to go keep him company when Dad turned and walked heavily toward the house.

Looking up, he saw Cass at the window. He smiled at his son, and Cass smiled back.

Despite the letter, or maybe because of it, Dad began to spend time alone with Cass. On rainy days, they ran experiments with the chemistry set. Cass had always known how to make carbon dioxide by mixing vinegar and baking soda. Dad taught him how to weigh the compounds on a finely calibrated scale, and how to catch the gas in a flask. On a Saturday trip to Duluth, they found a supply company where they bought litmus paper, sulphur and other chemicals.

Although the season was nearly over, they also began learning how to fish on the inland lakes. One sunny Saturday, after splitting firewood together all morning and half the afternoon, they drove back into the woods for miles with Mr. Benson. They portaged the canoe to a spruce-bordered lake and fished in silence until they had caught enough of the large-eyed, humpbacked walleyes for an ample Sunday dinner.

Except for the occasional eerie shriek of a loon, and the gentle slap of waves on their metal hull, and the plop of their lures in the water, the world was quiet. Nothing man-made disturbed the peace. When Cass saw a moose wading in the slanted sunlight among the lilypads on the far shore, he whispered, "There!" and pointed. The moose was too far away to bother with them, but Cass would no more have spoken loudly in this place than he would in church.

As if the moose had signaled the end of the day, they packed up their gear and carried the canoe back through the woods while they still had enough light to see. In the dusk, they tied the canoe to the top of the car, stowed their rods and tackleboxes, and climbed in.

The sun still shone behind a hill, where the road turned sharply to the left. At the crest of the hill, an enormous animal loomed into sight, as if it had risen out of the earth. The mist that had filled the valleys as they fished swirled around the creature's legs, blurring its outline, and diffusing the light so that the silhouetted animal glowed in a brilliant halo.

As they stared in silence, entranced, the creature whisked its great, sweeping tail. Eddies of mist puffed skyward. Cass could see that the beast was as white as a unicorn.

At last Dad whispered, "Am I seeing things, Munson, or is that a horse?"

"Ya, that's only a horse. She's a beaut, though, ain't she? Kai Nielsen, just down the road here, keeps a team for hauling timber and for pulling the other loggers' trucks out when they get mired. Claims his horses have four-wheel drive built right in. They run loose when he's not working them."

Another horse, a brown one, strode over the top

of the hill and stood beside the white one, looking down at the car. They flicked their manes in the haloed sunlight, galloped across the road with their tails high and streaming behind them, and disappeared into the woods.

Their wild energy thrilled Cass. Only a horse, Mr. Benson had said, but horses were as unexpected here as mythical creatures.

Far in the distance a freight train pulling another load of iron to the harbor whistled a mournful note.

"If that doesn't beat all," said Dad. "What a country this is, this strange mixture of wilderness and heavy industry. I feel as if I were trapped in a book of old tales where things don't match up." He shook his head. "A moose and a team of draft horses and a diesel train, all in the same woods! I wouldn't be surprised now to see a unicorn or a troop of Little People around that bend in the road."

"Dad," said Cass happily, "I thought of a unicorn, too."

"Cass and I always used to say the same thing at the same time," Dad explained to Mr. Benson. "Now we're thinking along the same track, too. Like son, like father."

Sitting in the middle, between the two big men, Cass leaned now against Mr. Benson, now against his father as they rounded curves. Feeling Dad's shoulder move as he steered, Cass enjoyed his sense of his father's size and power. The men's smell was a mixture of fresh fish, mosquito dope, and kerosene.

Cass breathed it in, feeling that he was one of them. He wished this evening, this happiness, could last.

They drove slowly along the narrow gravel road winding through the forest, and passed the several buildings known as Maryville. In the lumbering heyday, a village had thrived here, but now Mary Augustana was the only citizen. For comfort, or some other reason nobody understood, she kept a small fire going in her yard day and night, feeding it with maple trees she felled with an ax. She was there in the yard now, wearing a faded dress, with her white hair tucked under a baseball cap, chopping wood. Cass was surprised as always when he saw signs of people in the sparsely settled woods north of the lake.

Dad tooted a tentative soft toot, inviting a greeting. Mary thumbed her nose and turned her back.

"Why'd she do that?" said Cass. "We never did anything to hurt her."

"Don't take it personally," said Mr. Benson. "Mary don't like company."

After a moment, he added, "Our children went to school together in the old days. Mary used to be a kindly, laughing woman."

"I never knew you had children," said Cass.

"We both had sons, Mary and me." Mr. Benson cleared his throat loudly. "They both went down on the *Edmund Fitzgerald*."

"What's that?"

In the awkward silence, Dad said gently, "It was an ore boat that sank in a storm a few years back."

Glad nobody could see his flush of embarrassment in the deep twilight, Cass was grateful for Dad's pat on his knee.

None of them spoke again until Dad slowed the car at the wide place in the road called Reed. Over the door of one building hung a sign that said, BEER in red neon, PIZZA in blue; green neon framed the announcement.

"Munson," Dad said, "would you like to stop for some pizza and conviviality?"

Simultaneously, Cass said, "Dad, how about some pizza?"

They all laughed. "Like father, like son," said Cass.

"Don't know how pizza will set on a belly that's expecting fish," said Mr. Benson, "but I wouldn't mind a little glass of beer before bedtime."

The place was a crowded country café like Petersons', with living quarters visible through a curtained doorway. A couple of families eating supper, several men sitting alone on stools at the bar, and four noisy men at a table crowded the small room.

A woman in an apron, holding a crying toddler on her hip, said, "Here's a place, Munson."

"Munson," said the man behind the bar. "It's been a spell."

"Reed," Mr. Benson said, and nodded back.

Before she took their order, the woman called into the kitchen, "Betty, come and get your brother."

Cass recognized Betty from the schoolbus.

As they ate their pizza, heated in a microwave behind the bar, Cass sipped his milk and looked around the room at the mounted deer heads and stuffed lake trout and ducks frozen in flight on wooden plaques.

The four men at the table bragged louder and louder. One of them was disagreeing with the others. "Ah, you're all talk," he said.

"I'll show you," shouted another, a beefy man in a camouflage hunting hat, who shoved his chair back so harshly it tipped over backward. He stomped outdoors, leaving the chair on the floor.

"Yeah, show him," one of his friends yelled after him as the screen door slammed. All four of the men were dusty with coarse sawdust, which clung to their hair and whiskers and clothing. Pine pitch stiffened their denim jackets and caught the dirt.

"It's not much for eating with all this commotion, is it?" said Dad to Cass and Mr. Benson. "When you're ready, we'll leave." He moved his chair close to Cass.

"Ya," said Mr. Benson, smiling and rubbing his chin. "Too much conviviality to suit me."

Cass thought his friend looked diminished somehow, smaller and older and out of place. But he was too curious to leave now. "I want to see what they're talking about," Cass said.

"Ah, they're bragging. Mighty hunters, they are. Sportsmen." Mr. Benson spat the words.

All around them, people looked down at their plates, as if the loggers' loud talk had embarrassed them.

The man in the hat blustered back into the room carrying a heavy four-foot pipe with a wide, pointed blade welded to one end. He left the inside door standing open, despite the chill evening air.

"Put that thing away, Marsh Potter," said the bartender.

"This here's my bear stabber," said the man in the hat, ignoring him. "Ground me down a lawn-mower blade to make the knife."

He held the weapon horizontally by his side, like a spear, and turned toward the door. "What you do," he said, "is wait at the dump till one of them cusses come along, and then *zamm* — right in the brisket."

He threw the makeshift spear, which cut easily through the screen and reinforcing wire mesh of the outer door. The pipe clattered and echoed in the graveled parking lot.

Cass heard people all over the room catch their breath. The women sat nearer their children, watching out of the corners of their eyes. Dad and several other men stood up and moved in quickly on the man in the camouflage hat, who swayed unsteadily. Reed roared, "Out of here! This is a family place!"

The man who had said the others were all talk leaned back against the wall and picked his teeth with a paper matchbook, as if the noise had nothing to do with him.

His other two companions stood up unsteadily.

"Come on, Marsh," said one. "Let's go spear us some bear."

They propped up the man in the camouflage hat, and all three men slammed out through the damaged door. A moment later, spun gravel rapped the side of the building as they sped out of the lot in a four-wheel-drive vehicle with roll bars.

A woman got up and gently touched the jagged hole in the screen before closing the door, taking care not to make any noise. Cass saw Betty and her little brother, watching from the kitchen.

People cleared their throats and resumed eating. Cass felt like a stranger who had blundered into a family quarrel; their black sheep had thrown a tantrum, and the family would not be able to discuss it until the stranger left.

"Good pizza, Mrs. Reed." Dad handed Cass his jacket so that he stood automatically without being told.

They paid at the bar. "Evening, folks," said Dad to everyone in the room. "Good to see you all."

Back in the car, Mr. Benson said, "That Marsh Potter's a son of a gun."

"What were they talking about?" Cass mimicked Potter with contempt. " 'This here's my bear stabber! Let's go spear us some bear!' "

"Them fools got drunk last fall and went out to the dump," Mr. Benson said. "They speared this little bitty baby black bear, not more than a hundred pounds, that come in to eat the garbage. Like killing sitting ducks. They been bragging about it so much, by now you'd think the critter was a half-ton grizzly. Game warden's watching for them to try it again."

Cass remembered the four bears they'd seen at the dump. "I hate these people up here!" he said.

"Me?" Mr. Benson asked.

"Not you! You're not like the rest of them."

"I am, Cass. It's Marsh Potter who's not like most of us. Any other man and half the women in Reed's place can hunt circles around those louts. Reed himself could find the one deer in a ten-acre swamp. They hunt the way I fish, for meat on the table. They can't stand the guts of Marsh Potter, or anybody else who takes more than his share of the game, or brags, or hunts without skill."

"Some people drink a glass of beer with their supper," said Dad; "some get drunk. Some people are hunters; others are butchers."

"There's sheep, Cass," said Munson Benson, "and there's goats."

Maybe, thought Cass. But I've met hardly any sheep and a whole herd of goats since I came up here. And I could do without the lectures.

Seven

It seemed to Cass that years of school had passed before Thanksgiving came, and that the Wednesday before the holiday lasted for weeks. The teachers had promised not to assign homework, so Cass looked forward to a lazy vacation. He would be out in the woods at dawn every day, and when he got cold and had to come indoors, he would read *Huckleberry Finn* again.

At snack time that morning, he spilled half a pint of milk in his lap. He had to sit in soggy jeans and underwear and go hungry until lunch.

Meeting Cass at the pencil sharpener, Ansel sneered at the wet spot on Cass's pants. "You do need diapers, I see."

Cass jabbed at Ansel's arm with the point of his pencil, but Ansel twisted away and swaggered back to his seat, unscathed.

Cass's jeans dried stiff and had rubbed his legs raw by the time Mrs. Hubbard made the weekly lice check. She went down the rows quickly, parting each child's hair with one of his own pencils. When she came to Cass, she lifted a lock of his hair and was about to move on when she spotted something. She lifted another strand with the pencil. The other children began to snicker.

"Just a minute, Cass," she said. "I need my bifocals."

Cass wanted to evaporate in a puff of smoke and never return to earth again. He touched his scalp with his fingertips and felt the granular crystals in his hair.

Mrs. Hubbard put on the rhinestone-studded glasses she wore on a chain around her neck. She inspected his hair again, looking down her long, pinched nose.

"That's only sugar!" said Cass. "Ansel dumped a packet of sugar in my hair in the lunch room yesterday!"

"Well, they look like nits to me," said Mrs. Hubbard, standing at a distance.

She leaned toward Cass with the pencil held daintily between her thumb and forefinger, her pinky curled high in the air. "They certainly do. The nurse will have to check you before you can be readmitted to class."

Cass made his face smile. He swallowed the lump of tears in his throat, trying to keep them from rising into his eyes. He stared defiance into Ansel Peterson's grinning face as he walked out of the room and slammed the door.

When he returned, Cass had a note from the nurse folded up to the size of a matchbook. He walked to the teacher's desk, which stood at the front of the room on a little raised platform, and bowed to Mrs. Hubbard. Standing at arm's length, he presented the note to her, held between thumb and forefinger, with his pinky curled as she had curled hers earlier.

He gave her a courtly nod and a false smile. "Sugar," he said in a clear voice.

He could feel all the students holding their breath. Out of the corner of his eye, he saw the delight in Ansel's face.

As Mrs. Hubbard read the note, Cass returned to his seat.

Ansel leaned forward and whispered, "Way to go, Kennedy. You got the old turkey good that time. Look at her wattles shake. Look at the vein on her forehead stand up."

Mrs. Hubbard jammed the folded paper into her pocket. "Anyone can make a mistake," she said, absent-mindedly smoothing the little bulge the note made in her pocket. "We wouldn't want to all catch lice from Cass, would we, boys and girls?"

As he looked around the silent room, Cass could see the contempt for Mrs. Hubbard in his classmates' faces. His heart was beating hard from his perform-ance. He still felt the outrage of being falsely accused, but at the same time he thought he had earned some points in his classmates' book of respect. That was a first.

In science class, Mr. Ulseth continued his discussion of survival techniques which had begun that week. The science teacher took his eighth-grade students on a trip every summer, mountain climbing in the West. But he began preparing them early. In the woods that grew right to the edge of the playground, his fourth-grade students learned how to build a safe fire; how to avoid getting lost; how, if they did get lost, to find their way again.

By the time they reached the fifth grade, every student could identify wild foods, knew how to conserve body heat, and never went into the woods without a knife, a compass, and matches.

This week, Mr. Ulseth had read aloud Jack London's story "To build a Fire," about a trapper who, wild with panic after getting his feet wet in deadly winter, wasted his last matches and doomed himself.

For that day's class, Mr. Ulseth had assigned Cass the task of building a fire with wet wood. Hunched in their parkas and ski jackets against the cold wind off the lake, the class gathered around Cass at the edge of the playground.

"We won't have to soak your wood in a bucket, after all the rain we've had this week, Cass," said

Mr. Ulseth. "Explain what you're doing as you go along, now."

Cass set his red nylon backpack on a rock. "I'll gather all my wood first, so the fire won't go out while I hunt for logs," he said. "I'm looking for a couple of dead saplings that have fallen against other brush. That way they'll still be off the ground and dry. I don't want any logs that are rotting in the leaves."

"Come on, Ansel," said Mr. Ulseth, pointing with the stem of the pipe he still carried, even though he had quit smoking years ago. "Lend a hand."

Ansel kicked a rock and scuffed off with his hands in his pockets.

Brilliant orange berries hung from the mountain ash trees near the edge of the clearing, the magic rowans of Irish legend. After the rest of the color had died out, they festooned the bleak woods like beads and baubles until the birds ate them all. The trees were in constant motion now with the comings and goings of birds.

Every object in the woods was glazed with a thin coating of crackly ice that shimmered even on this cloudy day. As Cass passed between bushes, twigs bent and split the ice off like stiff, outgrown skin.

He found a dead birch, still standing erect, although most of its branches had fallen off. He began to push and pull it, trying to break it off near the ground.

"Hold it, Cass," Mr. Ulseth called.

Cass looked around as he whipped the birch back and forth, faster and faster.

"Cass! Whoa!" Mr. Ulseth shouted.

Just then, the birch tree, still standing upright, broke in midair. Cass had time only to throw his arms up to protect his head and neck as pieces of the broken tree trunk thudded all around him. One of them glanced off his shoulder and knocked him down.

An instant later Ansel reached him. "You all right?" he said, helping Cass stand.

Cass brushed himself with a show of toughness. "Yeah. But that thing nearly brained me." He looked around and saw that the piece of birch that had struck him was a log four feet long. It could have killed him.

"Where'd it hit you?" Mr. Ulseth said, talking around his pipe.

Cass gingerly felt a place on his back.

The teacher checked him over thoroughly, talking as he prodded. "Best demonstration I ever saw of what I was telling you last week. Dead birch rots. You're O.K., Cass?" Cass nodded.

Mr. Ulseth put his arm around the boy's shoulder. "Remember Robert Frost's poem? 'Three foggy mornings and one rainy day will rot the best birch fence a man can build.' Frost knew what he was talking about. Maybe he pulled a tree down on his head sometime."

66

Cass's feelings hurt even more than his shoulder.

"I know I did once," Mr. Ulseth went on. "That's how I happen to remember about rotten birch trees."

As they returned to the exposed rocks where Cass had decided to lay the fire, his classmates were quiet and serious. They helped him break the birch into manageable pieces.

Cass pulled a handful of sticks and bark from one of the big pockets of his parka. "I pick up tinder when I walk on the beach and carry it in my pockets," he said.

Mr. Ulseth nodded and stroked his beard. "Good idea. That driftwood's dry as bones. Your birch bark and spruce sticks are good, too."

"Here's a trick my dad showed me," said Cass.

He opened his backpack and removed a wad of steel wool and a dry-cell battery with caps taped over the terminals. He laid the steel wool at the edge of the tinder and arranged larger spruce sticks like a tepee over the dry bark and other tinder. Then he placed the broken pieces of birch like a log cabin around the kindling.

"You have to leave plenty of spaces between the pieces of wood so the flames can get oxygen," he said as he worked. "A box-shaped fire like this acts like a chimney. Air gets pulled in down here at the bottom and goes out the top."

As everybody leaned close to watch, Cass removed

the caps from the battery terminals. His mouth was dry. He knew he'd never live it down if this fire failed.

"The little wires of the steel wool get hotter than a match, and the wind doesn't blow out burning metal the way it does a match flame."

In demonstration of what he had said, he put the battery through an opening he had purposely left in the side of the firewood structure and touched both terminals to the steel wool.

As the electrical current flowed through the fuzzy metal, its tiny filaments of steel began to glow red hot. The tinder surrounding it caught fire. Cass withdrew the battery and blew gently on the flames. The spruce sticks began to burn furiously. The birch bark steamed and sizzled, and then it, too, caught. Awakened by the heat, a regiment of tiny insects fled from a hole in the end of one of the birch logs. Boiling water bubbled and fizzed behind them.

Despite the bitter wind, Cass felt beads of sweat trickle down the side of his face. Feeling triumphant, he stood up with a smile so big it hurt his face and said, "*Voilà!* A matchless fire."

"How does that work?" said Ben Brewer, hefting the battery in his hand.

Now that the tension was broken, everyone talked at once.

"It would be heavy in a backpack on a camping trip," said Jenny.

68

"Yeah, and who's going to have a dry cell on him every time he needs a fire?" said Ansel.

"If you were camping," said Cass, "you could take a lantern powered by a dry cell, and that wouldn't be much heavier than a big flashlight."

"That's cheating," Ansel persisted. "You're supposed to use matches, not some kind of . . . technology."

"No, Ansel," said Mr. Ulseth. "That's ingenuity. It's not as convenient a method as matches, but with wet wood, it's more reliable."

"Even matches are technology," said Ben.

"True," Mr. Ulseth continued. "On average, we get more than one hundred and fifty days of below-freezing temperature in Minnesota, every year. At thirty below zero, the outdoors is sixty-some degrees colder than your refrigerator. We need all the help we can get!"

Cass imagined himself telling Dad tonight how he had carried tinder with him, how he had found a standing birch to assure that the wood was dry, how the trick Dad had taught him with the battery had worked like a charm. He would tell Dad his pun about the matchless fire, and Dad would laugh until his stomach ached.

"Look," said Ben, pointing at the fire. Now that the dry tinder and bark and spruce gum had burned away, the birch was beginning to smoke and the flame was dampening.

Cass stooped over and blew on his fire until he felt lightheaded and faint, but as soon as he stopped to catch his breath, the flame snuffed out, and smoke engulfed him.

"That's all right, Cass," Mr. Ulseth said. "If everything worked just right, our experiments wouldn't be like life. Cass has taught us a lesson that could save our lives sometime — rotten birch doesn't amount to much. Let's add some hardwood while we've still got coals from your good tinder and kindling."

Except for the birch and spruce, all of the trees looked alike to Cass. Ansel, however, moved with certainty to a dead sapling that had fallen into brush, which held it above the ground. He tugged it out of the tangle, deftly broke off twigs, and laid them on the small pile of coals the kindling had made.

"Ah," said Mr. Ulseth. "A nice maple."

As Ansel's twigs burst into flame, he replaced the rotten birch logs with pieces of the brittle maple trunk. The fire and Cass's anger burned hotter and hotter. Once again, Ansel had stolen his thunder.

But Ansel turned to Cass and said in a friendly way, "Don't take it hard. I've been building fires since I was a little kid."

For less than an instant, Cass felt grateful to Ansel. Then he remembered the months of razzing. Hardening his heart, Cass turned and walked away alone.

Eight

On his way back to Mrs. Hubbard's classroom for math, Cass hung his backpack on his labeled hook in the hallway. Double-checking the battery to be sure the caps were securely taped on both terminals, he could hear Mr. Maxwell's voice in the principal's office across the hall.

"I'm calling your parents now. If you continue to fight, you'll be suspended."

Cass imagined Old Maximum's mustache twitching, as it always did when he was furious. He wondered who was catching it.

Three younger boys filed silently out of the office, the Erickson twins and another third-grader who lived up the lake. Cass avoided their eyes; if they knew he had overheard their scolding, they would be mad at him for knowing.

In class, Cass tried to concentrate on the interminable page of long-division problems.

Thirty-eight goes into three hundred and seventeen, he thought, curling a strand of hair around his finger again and again — nine?

He calculated nine times thirty-eight. "Rats! It's eight."

"Quiet, Cass," said Mrs. Hubbard.

He had spoken aloud without meaning to. Outdoors in the woods, a cardinal whistled sweetly. Nibbling on the cedar twig that he carried in his pocket, Cass stared out the window. He leaned his jaw on his fist and watched the activity around Mr. Ulseth's bird station. A piece of suet hung in a wire basket on a high, flimsy branch, where the nuthatches and juncos could reach it, but the bears could not. Chickadees and one downy woodpecker came and went with quick darting movements. A chipmunk sat on the station's roof, cracking sunflower seeds.

Cass thought of the squirrels that lived in the spruces between the cabins at home. After weeks of patient coaxing, two of them had begun to take food from his hand. He decided to mark one with India ink, so he could tell them apart.

Suddenly Cass heard loud voices in the hall and, almost simultaneously, smelled pungent smoke as the fire alarm went off.

"Line up," said Mrs. Hubbard, snapping her fingers even though the students were already forming an orderly line at the door. The bell, just outside in the corridor, was so loud Cass put his hands over his ears as he passed it. Through the crowd of children, he glimpsed Mr. Maxwell and a lower-grade teacher, stooped over something on the floor.

The junior high students who had been taking

72

showers when the bell rang filed out through the double doors to the playground in their stocking feet, and with damp clothes and dripping hair. Cass saw Eileen among them. Nobody had been able to stop for coats or hats or boots or mittens. The girls gathered shivering in close groups, clinging together with their arms around each other for warmth. The boys shifted from one foot to another with their shoulders hunched and their hands in their pockets.

"They plan these fire drills for cold weather just to torture us," said Todd.

"This is no drill," said Ben. "Didn't you smell the smoke?"

"Old Maximum was all excited about something in the hall by the coats when I came back from the bathroom," said Todd.

"Leave it to Toad to be there when trouble strikes," said Ben. "He always knows who's in trouble, but he's never to blame."

"I think Ansel's it this time," said Todd.

"I think so, too," said Ben. "He was fooling around with Cass's backpack when I came late to class. Where is Ansel, anyway?"

Cass was furious that Ansel had been messing with his things. But another thought overrode his anger.

"I bet it was my battery!" said Cass.

"That's shocking!" said Ben with an English accent.

Cass could hear his heart thud in his ears. Maxwell

is going to kill me, he thought. And if he doesn't, Dad will. Dad had forgiven the schoolbus fight, but not even Dad could forgive a thing like this.

The all-clear sounded as Cass searched his mind for hiding places. He wanted to crawl into a hole and pull the hole in after him. If only he were wearing his parka, he thought with half-hearted bravado, he would hitchhike to Canada. He tried to make himself small and inconspicuous among the other boys as they filed back to their classes, but he was half a head taller than most of them, and Mr. Maxwell was waiting for him.

"March yourself into my office," said the principal from across the hall, punching toward Cass with his index finger.

"Why does such a young guy always sound like my grandmother?" Cass muttered.

"He looks like his face caught fire," Ben said with a laugh.

But Cass knew that this was no laughing matter. He had heard his parents talking quietly at home about Mr. Maxwell, about his pink, manicured hands and his tidy ideas. He was especially hard on boys, they thought, who were so unlike his own perfect, doll-like daughter.

But nobody could be tolerant about a fire in a school, Cass realized as he faced Mr. Maxwell. Children might have been killed. Cass could see his own shirt pulse over his pounding heart.

"You evacuated the school, Kennedy," said Mr.

74

Maxwell, running his fingers through his curly gray hair. His face and ears were bright red. "What happened?"

"I don't know. I was in my class figuring three-seventeen divided by thirty-eight when the alarm went off." Facing the door, Cass could see Ben skulking in the hallway.

"I found the battery in your knapsack, hanging on your hook. I found it *after* I put out the fire in your papers." He thrust a sheaf of charred papers at Cass.

Cass accepted the papers without looking at them. "I had the battery for Mr. Ulseth's class," he said. "I've been in Mrs. Hubbard's class all hour."

"All right, Cass, it's only fair to check the facts. You can appreciate, though, that I'm nervous about fire after the one we had in the storeroom last month."

Ben knocked on the door as he came into the office. "Cass didn't do it, Mr. Maxwell. I saw Ansel playing around with Cass's battery a few minutes before the alarm rang."

Mr. Maxwell turned as Ansel barged through the open door behind Ben.

Ansel's face was pale. "It was an accident," he said. "I was only trying to see how it worked, the battery. The steel wool started to burn and dropped onto Cass's papers, and they caught on fire. I put the fire out, though."

Cass was amazed. Ansel could have tried to let me take the blame, he thought. The anger he had felt about Ansel's snooping in his backpack was forgotten now.

"The fire was still burning when I got there," said Mr. Maxwell. "You know the floors in this building are wood. Imagine yourselves trapped in Mrs. Hubbard's room by a fire in the corridor." The principal's hands were trembling.

Cass dreaded what Dad would say when he found out about this mess. He might put an end to the fishing trips and the chemistry experiments, on the grounds that Cass was too irresponsible for such grown-up activities. That was the direction Dad's lectures usually took.

Mr. Maxwell turned to Cass. "You're responsible, too, Cassidy, for bringing that incendiary device to school."

Cass shook his head in disbelief. "I brought it for a demonstration in science class. I was careful to tape the caps on the terminals the way my dad showed me."

"I'll check the facts with Mr. Ulseth. Unless he can explain, there will be a letter placed in your permanent records. The two of you will have to split the cost of damage to school property. In the meantime, Ansel, since you started the fire, you're in detention in this office until your parents come for a conference."

"How much damage is there?" asked Ansel.

"A couple of hundred dollars," said Mr. Maxwell.

"The fire was an accident," said Cass. "Ansel

76

shouldn't be blamed the same as if he had set it on purpose."

Ansel looked at Cass, open-mouthed.

"Accident or not, the effect would have been the same if the fire had gotten out of hand," said Mr. Maxwell.

"Cass didn't do it," said Ansel. "It isn't fair to make him pay."

Cass loked at Ansel as if he had never seen him before.

"You both share the responsibility," said Mr. Maxwell.

"Ansel was only trying to see how the electricity worked," said Cass.

"You're loyal friends, boys, I'll say that for you," said Mr. Maxwell. If you only knew, thought Cass. "Now you two go back to class," the principal said.

Cass and Ben exchanged a thumbs-up sign with Ansel as they left him in the office.

"Thanks; you didn't have to get me off the hook," said Cass in the hall. Feeling tears forming somewhere in his chest, he changed the subject. "Look at this."

He handed the partly burned papers to Ben. "A whole week's math homework. I forgot to hand it in."

Ben groaned.

"That finishes me for Thanksgiving vacation. It'll take all weekend to do it over. And what am I going to tell my folks? My dad's been mad at me all summer; we were just patching it up." Cass wiped his hands, black with soot and charred paper, on his pants.

"You didn't do anything wrong," Ben said. "Ulseth will vouch for you."

"Yeah. But how will I come up with a hundred dollars?"

"Will he whip you, your dad?"

"Naw. He'll just make me squirm. He'll ground me for the weekend, if not for the rest of my life. He'll make me work off the damage."

But it wasn't the work, nor even Dad's certain anger, that bothered Cass. He felt ashamed. He wasn't a little boy anymore, Dad had said. Yet, no matter how Cass tried, he messed up. He could stand anger by getting angry in return, but Dad's disappointment in him was unbearable.

Cass examined the shelf over his coat hook. The varnish on the edge of the wood had burned black. Two planks would have to be replaced, sanded and varnished, and the wall would need paint. The heat had melted a hole in the sleeve of his parka, right through the puffy insulation and lining.

Cass put his forefinger through the hole. "Maximum will never let me forget this. My permanent record!"

"He'll put a big red sticker on your folder." Ben laughed. " 'Firebug,' it'll say."

Nine

By the time the schoolbus reached Kennedy's Resort, Cass had decided what to do.

Following Eileen out the door of the bus, he nodded at Ansel and Ben, who were sitting together in the front seat.

Ansel gave him thumbs up.

"Good luck," said Ben.

"Don't I hope."

Mrs. Larson waited with the red lights of the bus flashing and the STOP flap open, while Cass and Eileen crossed the empty highway. They turned and waved to their friends.

"What's this?" said Eileen. "You and Ansel Peterson, bosom buddies?"

"Oh, he's not so bad, I guess."

"I heard that Ansel started that fire today with your battery."

The metal resort sign rattled in the breeze.

"Yeah. And Maxwell wants to know why I'm

bringing 'incendiary devices' to school. Dad's going to pop his cork."

"If it wasn't your fault, he'll understand that."

"That's what you say. He's never mad at you."

I'm the one Dad will ground for the whole vacation, Cass thought to himself. I'm the one who will be told for the eleventy-seventh time to grow up and take responsibility.

The thin glaze of ice in the woods had melted as the afternoon warmed a bit. The sun would set earlier every day until late in December, when night would fall well before suppertime. On cloudy days like this one, the sun might as well never have risen, for all the cheer it brought. The road through the trees to the Kennedys' house and cabins was as damp and gloomy as Cass's spirits.

"I have to get something in here," Cass said when they came to the storage shed. "I'll be along in a minute."

Cass watched through the shed window until Tongue bolted out of the house, almost knocking Eileen down. Cass whistled to the dog as he dumped his books out of his knapsack onto the workbench. Tongue dashed into the shed while Cass was pulling his camping equipment out of the wooden chest.

"Sit," he said firmly to the prancing dog. "I'll pet you later. We have to hurry now."

Mr. Maxwell had confiscated the dry-cell battery at school, but Cass quickly found the spare, put it in the lantern, and zipped it, along with a canvas ground cloth, into his empty knapsack. On impulse, he also snapped into the game pouch of his parka the anchor light Mom carried on the boat for safety in the summer; it had belonged to Grandpa Cassidy. He tied the shoelace on his compass to a belt loop and slipped it into his jeans pocket; he checked his other pocket for his jackknife and matches. His old knot-tying rope was still in that pocket, too.

He had already written the note in class while Mrs. Hubbard, off on a tangent, had talked about the desolation of the moon. Now he tore the note out of his tablet and put it under a hammer on top of his math text, so it couldn't blow away. Before leaving, he read it one more time.

> Dear Mom and Dad,
>   I'm sorry about the fire at school. Don't worry about me and please don't come after me until I'm ready. I am nothing like I will be when I grow up.
>
> > Your son,
> > Cassidy Kennedy

He found a pencil stub and added a postscript: "Tongue's with me." Beside his name, he drew a lopsided heart.

He imagined Dad calling for him, searching up and down the road, telephoning neighbors. Perhaps he would be sorry he had hounded his boy.

Dad's the one who's always after me to grow up,

Cass thought; I'll show him I can make it on my own. He's the one who's never satisfied; I'll show him. After he's over being mad, I'll come back. Maybe tomorrow, in time for Thanksgiving dinner.

Carrying his rolled sleeping bag lashed to his backpack, Cass skirted the lawn. He stayed out of sight in the woods until he and Tongue came to the cliff above the beach. There they ran across the lichen-covered rock between sparse stands of trees, avoiding both the tangled woods and the icy beach where frozen spray glazed every surface. Out on the lake, as far as Cass could see, the foaming crests of waves curled upon themselves and plunged into the troughs, to rise and curl and foam again, like a thousand horses' arching necks.

By the time Cass reached the cave, the dusk was deepening into night. He could hear the big rolling waves break against the cliff face below, but he was too busy to watch them. Tongue trotted out of sight as Cass lit one of the candles he had stored in glass jars. In its light, he built a small fire at the mouth of the cave with wood from the pile inside. He stacked rocks on the far side of the fire to reflect its heat into the cave.

Tongue whined, and Cass coaxed him around the side of the fire into the cave.

"It must be half past suppertime, the way my stomach feels," Cass said aloud.

In the dim candlelight, he pried off the cover of the potato chip container and poured the food onto his canvas ground cover, leaving the old clothes in the bottom. He set the alphabet soup, opened with the punch on his jackknife, beside the fire.

As always, he had been tempted to test his dad's warning, but resisted the temptation. If a can were put on a fire unopened, Dad said, the contents would expand until the can exploded with the force of a bomb; the explosion could demolish a kitchen.

When the soup began to bubble, Cass pulled it away from the fire with a forked stick. He ate with the spoon on his jackknife. Tongue begged for his share, so Cass split the sausages and shoestring potatoes and the dried beef with the dog. The salty food made Cass so thirsty, he drank his root beer and all of the orange juice except one can. Despite being stored in the depths of the cave, the contents were slushy; the liquid had begun to freeze. He saved two chocolate bars for morning.

After supper Cass had nothing to do but eat and read, feed the fire, and pet Tongue. He took off his shoes and snuggled down into his sleeping bag, after shaking it to be sure that no rattlesnakes or black widows had set up housekeeping inside. The books all said that no rattlesnake species ranged this far north, but he wasn't taking any chances.

Nibbling the last of the raisins, he thought with satisfaction that nobody would make him brush his teeth tonight. His final swallow of orange juice tasted as sour as lemons.

Cass leaned against the wall of the cave, holding

a candle close to his book. Wax dripped on the pages of his favorite Irish fairly tale, the one about the Red Man who, for a price, could restore the dead to life. At the end of each paragraph, he peered across the fire, trying to see the bears and timber wolves that might be gathering in the darkness beyond. Tongue snored, his head heavy in the boy's lap.

The candle had burned down almost to the end. The flame began to burn his fingertips, so Cass lit another, dripped wax on a ledge of rock, and lodged the fresh candle upright in the soft wax. The wind was loud in the trees now, mingling with the rhythmic crash of the waves below. Nearby, two trees rubbed against each other and made a weird, screeching noise, keening above the sound of the wind and water. Cass had always wished he could see the lake from inside the cave. Now he was glad that the entrance faced downshore. As the northeast wind whooped past, only wayward gusts found him in this haven, and the wind swept most of the smoke away.

Snow hissed as it struck hot rocks near the fire. Cass risked leaving the cave to look around. Out in the open, away from the lee of the rock, the wind was visible now, a solid force of gritty snow flung into his face. He could see no sky, no lake, no woods, no ground beneath his feet — only a wall of hurled snow on every side. He could hear it strike his hood and could feel it pelt his face. This first big blizzard of the winter promised to be a doozy.

He wished for the comfort of light. In Minneapolis, when the neighborhood gathered to play kick-the-can, sneaking behind houses and between garages, he had always been just around the corner from a street light or only a lawn away from a bright kitchen window. The night sky always glowed with the reflected lights of the city. Cass had been able to see bright constellations like Orion, but not the unnumbered pricks of starlight that were visible here on clear nights.

Here on the North Shore, he often lay in the damp grass on an August night and counted dozens of meteors in an hour. He could see stars with the naked eye that hadn't been visible from his Minneapolis yard even with a telescope. But on cloudy moonless nights, when the only lights were fireflies flashing their mating signals, he never went far from the cabins without gritting his teeth to hold back the terror of the black, blind night.

He put a thick log on the fire, grateful for the comfort of its heat and light, but beginning to worry that his wood might not last as long as he had hoped in such a wind.

The snuffle of a bear or the howl of wolves would be inaudible with the shriek of the wind in his ears, he thought. But bears hibernate; wolves would stay at home in a storm like this. He smiled, imagining a family of wolves sitting, their knees crossed, in easy chairs by a fire, playing poker on the coffee table to while away the time. The mother wolf would be wearing the father's bathrobe over her sweater and jeans, like Mom —

That's what his own family would be doing tonight, Cass thought — sitting around the fire listening to the Duluth radio station, reading, playing Monopoly, eating popcorn and spiced cider. He wished he were at home with them, even if Eileen owned hotels on Boardwalk. He felt guilty, knowing they must be worried about him.

The flames licked the new log, enveloped it, and then leaped up. Cass crawled back into his cool sleeping bag. Watching the shadows flicker on the walls of the cave, he wondered whether any bats were hibernating in there with him. In a book at school, he had seen a picture of a woman whose swollen toes had been bitten by a vampire bat. Somewhere he had read that, far from medical care, bat-bitten fingers or toes should be cut off. Or had he dreamed that? Cass shuddered.

Tongue roused to give Cass an absent-minded lick on the cheek, groaned a loud, contented groan, and closed his eyes again.

"We should have named you Stomach," said Cass. "Greedyguts."

Cass groaned, too, but he was not contented. His food was almost gone; he wondered whether somebody had stolen part of it. And already his big pile of wood had dwindled noticeably. He should have hidden in one of the cabins. Better yet, he should have faced the music.

The ground cloth under him kept the dampness away, but not the cold, and it didn't soften the ground. He wished for Bill the pillow, the bear he and Mom had sewn, way back when he was a little boy, four years old. He still liked to look at Bill, sitting on his bookshelves staring into space with button eyes, or soft and pudgy under the covers.

Trying to find a soft place in the stone floor, Cass rested his head on his arm and pulled Tongue against his own curved body. He covered his ear with the edge of the down sleeping bag, but he could not shut out the noise of the wind.

He began to wish he had not run away on so stormy a night. Dad and Mom would be out looking for him, worried sick, maybe lost themselves. But how would he ever get home in a storm like this? And if he did make it back, how would he explain what he had done?

Ten

Awakening suddenly, Cass cracked his head against something hard. Had he got turned around in his bed and bumped the corner of his dresser? He felt the cold bulge of rock that had done the damage and remembered that he was not in his soft bed at home, but here in the cave. Tongue stood over him, whining — or was it a wolf? — no, it was Tongue, whining and nosing at him.

The fire had burned out, leaving only a bed of glowing coals which gave little light. The wind howled louder than ever.

Tongue pawed at him, and Cass shoved him away in groggy confusion. "Back off, dog. What's the matter with you?"

He felt around in the dark for his jar of candles. Remembering that his matches were dwindling, like the food and the firewood, he lit a twig in coals and used that to light a candle. Carefully, he laid more logs on the fire.

All the while Cass worked, the dog pranced and

whined. He was twitching his ears as he did when the foghorn and ships' whistles blew, although Cass could hear nothing over the howling wind. Cass stretched his stiff muscles and wondered what time it was.

"How come you got me up when I just barely started to sleep?"

Tongue whined again and moved uneasily about the cave. He turned to make sure Cass was watching, then went outside into the wind and snow.

"All right," said Cass. "I'm coming."

He hurriedly laced his boots, fastened his parka hood and muffler over his nose and mouth so only his eyes were exposed, and pulled his down mittens over his cuffs. Tongue was waiting for him just beyond the mouth of the cave.

The snow swirled in gusts around Cass, now so thick his lantern beam penetrated the whiteness only a few feet ahead, now clearing momentarily. In a blizzard last winter, when the snow had stopped falling, the wind still swept it off the ground and kept it alive in the air.

In the clear moments, Cass saw enormous waves regularly surmounting the cliff face, swamping the lip of rock where he had stood to throw stones last summer. Sometimes a tongue of water swept in as far as the Norway pine where he had placidly eaten his breakfast of apple slices. The pine and every other object were covered with ice.

"This lake ain't no millpond," Cass said to himself, remembering Mun Benson's mild understatement.

He was aware of the restless dog bustling away and returning to his side. He felt the bump on his head throbbing. Yet he stood amazed, watching the waves fling geysers of water high in the air, feeling their thunder in his feet.

No wonder these rocks are scoured almost bare, he thought; how can even the orange lichen and blue harebells survive such punishment?

Momentarily the air cleared between Cass and the lake, and for an instant he saw a light offshore.

No, he thought. Couldn't be. Ships can't come that close. Lightning, maybe, playing tricks on my eyes.

But there was the flash again. Not lightning. Maybe a ship, Cass thought, making one of those famous last November trips the sailors talked about. So many sailors had died in so many late November gales on the Great Lakes that shipping companies sometimes paid extra to make up a crew for a late trip. It was in November, Dad had said, when the *Lafayette* went down, and again when the *Edmund Fitzgerald* sank.

A ship's light where no ship would dare to come, Cass knew. It must be signaling for help. But what could a boy alone with a dog in the swooping snow do for a foundering ship?

He thought of getting Mr. Benson — he would know what to do. But the fisherman's place was half a mile down the beaten shore, half a mile open to the gale. He decided instead to follow the logging road to the highway and telephone the Coast Guard from Petersons'. That route would be shorter and sheltered part of the way by the woods.

Tongue bounded to him when he called. In the big side pocket of his parka, Cass found the short rope he had used for practicing knots, and tied it to the dog's collar. Together, they began picking their way downshore, staying well back from the edge to avoid being swept away by a sudden wave.

As he clutched the rope with one hand and the lantern with the other, Cass's jaws ached from gritting his teeth. I place all heaven with its power, he said in his mind, and the night with its darkness, and the snow with its starkness, and the winds with their swiftness along their path.

According to the legend, Saint Patrick had blessed his people and given them the power to change into deer, enabling them to escape pursuers. He would need the sensitivity of a deer to make it through this night, he thought, when the night itself was the enemy, and the snow.

With the northeast wind at his back, the snow swept across the bare rocks before him. He saw in the lantern light that several inches had fallen, but the wind had driven it into deep drifts.

Tongue had set aside all of his clownishness. Now, with the firm decision of a lead sled dog, he took Cass on their accustomed path toward the point where the old logging road stopped at the edge of the woods. All the while the dog stayed well back from the ice-glazed cliff.

Cass could feel as much as hear the heavy waves breaking on the cliffs off to his left. Once Tongue plunged up to his neck in drifted snow. After that he avoided the smooth white pools and picked his way instead across broken rock where patches were swept bare.

Even with the lantern beam focused one step ahead of Tongue, Cass tripped on a rock he hadn't noticed and fell like a great bag of bones, bruising his hip. He was grateful for his leather boots, laced halfway up his calf, which saved him from turning his ankles on the uneven ground. With the wind bullying, shoving, sometimes almost lifting him off the ground, he had to lean backward or fall on his face.

At last, Tongue cut to the right, guided them to the edge of the woods, and backtracked a few yards.

"There it is," Cass shouted when he saw the strange forked spruce that marked the logging road. "You should have been a seeing-eye dog, Tongue."

But the wind whipped his words down the shore, out of his own hearing, and stole his breath away.

After the sight of the forked pine, every object and turn in the old logging road looked unfamiliar. The snow softened angles and edges. Tree trunks loomed up in the lantern beam, shaggy with shadow, brooding like huddled trolls. Outside the magic circle of light, the crowded trees dissolved, no longer distinguishable as separate objects.

Here, with the trees breaking the gale, the snow had not drifted much. In most places, it was only calf-deep, but that was deep enough. Cass tripped on rocks, stumbled over fallen logs, got tangled in briars, and fell into holes in the ground.

His legs were aching and bruised when he and Tongue struggled up the embankment to the wind-whipped highway at last. Facing into the wind toward Ansel's place, he could not see Petersons' neon store sign, nor any lights in the windows, nor the yard light above the gravel driveway. Those lights were usually left burning all night.

He couldn't see much past his own feet, in fact, so he found the edge of the road and followed it to the right. Petersons' place would be there, unless he had taken the wrong logging road through the woods. He looked at the compass he carried in his pocket, but the needle swung wildly in his shaking hand, and he couldn't tell which way was north.

Now he leaned forward into the wind to remain upright. Surely the Petersons had not turned off their lights on such a stormy night. Perhaps he had missed their place. Perhaps he was on the wrong road now, heading north into the wilderness. Perhaps the light he had seen on the lake was an illusion or lightning, and he would die in the snow for nothing.

Eleven

The bridge of Cass's nose and his cheeks no longer stung, but now were numb. He pulled his picky old mohair muffler around his face the way his mother always had when he was small. The wind had discovered a three-cornered tear where a tree limb had snagged the hole burned in his parka sleeve. His arm was cold, but he could feel sticky sweat on his back from the effort of standing erect in the gale.

Tongue was limping, but Cass was afraid to stop and rest. He had read too many stories of hunters marooned in blizzards who fell asleep and froze to death only a few steps from their dooryards. He had forgotten to bring a hatchet with him for building a lean-to or digging a trench. Unprepared to survive the cold, he had to find shelter.

As he waded through the snow that filled every dip in the road, and searched for a glimpse of bare pavement, only his next step mattered. He began to think about burrowing into a drift for shelter, but he had forgotten to bring a candle to heat a snow cave.

Suddenly Cass stumbled, shocked and alert, as if he had awakened while sleepwalking. Tongue had stopped to listen. Cass smelled woodsmoke. He was standing in Petersons' gravel driveway; he saw a light shimmer for an instant as the wind paused and gathered fury.

He waded up the steps of the wooden porch, making muffled hollow noises, and almost fell into the room when Ansel opened the door before he knocked.

"Tongue!" said Ansel. "Is that you, Cass? What are you doing out in a storm like this?"

As Ansel sputtered questions, he unzipped Cass's parka, pulled it off, and shook a cascade of ice and snow onto the linoleum. Cass slid down onto the floor with his back against the wall. Ansel handed him a steaming mug of coffee.

Warming his hands on the crockery, breathing in the steam and sipping the coffee, Cass looked round the room. On one wall, as he remembered, stood a bar, with rows of bottles reflected in a huge mirror. A gasoline lantern sputtered on the bar, illuminating a sign that said HOT DOGS in red letters. On the opposite wall, he could see a commercial refrigerator and shelves of groceries. The Petersons lived in the back of the store, through the shadows at the end of the bar. Cass closed his eyes, and his thoughts drifted.

"Where have you been, Cass?" Ansel's voice

sounded far away. "Your mother's out in this storm looking for you."

Ansel shook Cass's shoulders and splashed hot coffee on his leg.

Remembering the light he had seen on the lake, Cass stood up. "I've got to get my dad. There's a ship foundering east of Benson's point. Where's the phone?"

"Are you kidding? The phone has been out since suppertime, along with the electricity. When I heard you were missing, I couldn't get hold of anybody to tell them where I thought you were."

Cass stared at Ansel. "What made you think you knew? Where's my dad?"

"He's down at the power station with my folks and everyone else; that station stood there safe for forty years, my dad said, but the surf took out one wall tonight. They're trying to save the rest of the building with sandbags."

"Where's my mother? I've got to get help. That ship —"

"What ship? Before the power went out, the radio said that there's an ore boat on the reef at Isle Royale and another ship in distress off Castle Danger. But you couldn't have seen a ship in this storm."

"I did, though! Where's my mother?"

"Gee, Cass. She's up and down the road trying to find out where you went."

"Isn't anybody here?" said Cass.

"I am," snapped Ansel. "Liv's at your place with

Eileen. I'm supposed to take care of things here. Everybody else left before I heard you were missing."

"As you can see, I'm not missing!"

"You're lucky, then. That was a dumb thing you did, Cass, going off by yourself at this time of year, and nobody knowing. There are always storms —"

In the shadows, a chair scraped on the linoleum. A man Cass hadn't noticed was leaning on a table peering between beer bottles at Cass. He looked familiar somehow.

"Ain't you the kid who hunts bear with six-shooters?" The laughter in the man's throat changed to a wheezy cough. "Now you're the Coast Guard, too. Big talker, ain't you?"

"Don't say anything," said Ansel in a low voice. "That's Marsh Potter, Magda's father. He came after the power station called for help."

Cass had never been so tired. His arms and legs felt weighted. But he knew that the ship he had seen was nearing calamity, like the *Lafayette*, which still littered the shore with debris like his rusty chain all these years after the 1905 wreck.

"If there's no way to get the Coast Guard, I'll have to go back myself. Can you let me have some rope?" said Cass.

"Don't be such a jerk! This isn't a TV show. What are you going to do, lasso the boat?"

"Just get the rope." Cass pulled his damp parka on and zipped it up. The truth was, Cass had no definite plans for the rope, but he could never admit that to Ansel.

"No. I won't do it," said Ansel. "If you weren't so green, you'd understand how dangerous these gales are."

"Come on, Tongue." The dog came from behind the stove. Cass looped his short rope through the ring of the collar again and jammed his hands into his mittens. "I'm going, rope or no rope. Try and get some help for the ship, Ansel."

When he went out the door, the wind nearly swept Cass off the porch. At least it would be at his back now, he thought as he plunged into the storm again.

Standing at the edge of the highway, he looked northeast toward home and south toward the power plant. If desire could have conjured them, headlights would have loomed in the darkness.

His parents would have taken him in their arms and told him what to do. They would have tucked him in his bed and kissed his eyelids. They would have known how to save the ship. He imagined Mom, stalled in a ditch because of him. He saw the surf at the power plant lapping at Dad's ankles, breaking across his knees, but he stuffed the frightful thoughts into a back closet of his mind.

Struggling back toward the old logging trail, he thought he heard a shout on the wind. Ansel was floundering through the snow behind him, trying to hold the gas lantern high and steady as he slipped and slid. Cass waited for him to catch up.

"I'm going with you," Ansel shouted, shifting the coil of nylon rope he carried on one shoulder. He shifted his backpack. "I brought a sharp hatchet, matches, and a compass."

Cass gestured at the lantern and shouted close to Ansel's ear. "How will Magda's father see to drink?"

Ansel laughed and nodded. "Maybe he'll go home before he gets snowed in at our place and we get stuck with him for the weekend."

Now that he knew where he was, Cass thought the way seemed shorter. When they turned onto the logging road, Ansel pulled at his coat, signaling him to stop.

"I can't keep up with that dog," he shouted.

Ansel tied one end of the rope around Cass's waist and pulled the coil over his own shoulders and down around his chest. They wasted no more energy in talk, but nodded and clapped each other on the back in mutual encouragement before going on again.

Soon Cass felt a tug on the rope. Ansel had fallen. The hot globe of the lantern had shattered when it hit the snow. Ordinarily, Tongue would have pounced on Ansel and licked his face, seeing every event as an invitation to play. Instead he stood and waited solemnly while Cass took Ansel's hand and pulled him to his feet. They left the broken lantern beside the trail. Now they would have to depend on Cass's feeble battery lamp.

By the time they had struggled back through the woods to the forked spruce, Ansel and Cass were panting as hard as Tongue. Cass doubled up with pain in his side. Ansel knelt by a boulder, gasping into his mittens. Cass imitated him, trying to warm the searing air he breathed. Tongue leaned against the rock, too, with his head down.

"Now what?" screamed Cass when he had caught his breath. "It's worse all the time!"

"We'll never make it back to our place," Ansel shouted in his ear. "We've got to find the cave and build a fire."

Cass was astonished to hear Ansel mention the cave, but he didn't have time now to worry about that. He shielded his eyes from the wind and strained to see the lake. No lights were visible. With every wave that cracked against the cliff, a fountain shot high into the air. The wind drove the spray like freezing rain, so thick that the boys could not see past the edge of the cliff.

"I've got a fire," Cass shouted, gesturing upshore. Ansel nodded. They inched over the icy rocks, but all three at once lost their footing on the slick rocks and tumbled against each other in a bruised heap. They lay there, trying to gather the strength to crawl back into the woods.

With his head on the ground, Cass felt a grumbling, grinding vibration, like the sound of an iron giant eating rocks. Cass and Ansel sat up and looked closely at each other's faces, gesturing with their hands at their ears.

Now that he had felt the vibration in his flesh and

bone, Cass could hear it too, a clashing above the constant clatter of the freezing spray against his hood, the howling undertone of the wind, the rhythmic roar of the water. It must be the ship, grinding against the cliff.

Tongue's ears were pricked and his nose was up, sniffing the wind.

Cass put his mouth by the dog's big floppy ear. "Get him, Tongue," he said — the command he used when they were spooking rabbits and chipmunks in the woods.

Tongue's claws enabled him to grip the slippery rocks. He picked his way slowly upshore, toward the cave, with the boys crawling behind him on their hands and knees. Cass still held the makeshift leash, and he was still tied to Ansel with the rope around their waists.

Tongue stopped and growled and then strained against the leash, leading the boys closer to the leaping spray, forcing Cass to stow the feeble lantern in the game pouch of his parka, where it clanked against the anchor light. As they paused, Ansel crept to Tongue's side and put his arm around the dog's shoulder.

Tongue smelled the wind and lunged ahead past a stunted pine, with the boys scrambling, crawling, dragging alongside. And there, a few yards from the edge of the cliff, lay a man, face down. He was as still as if he were frozen to the rock.

Twelve

Cass got the lantern out again and shone the light on one bare foot. He and Ansel heaved the man over on his back. An ice-covered spruce twig poked through the torn breast pocket of his coat — a red coat, Cass saw — as jaunty as a flower in a lapel.

"Who is it?" shouted Ansel.

Unwillingly, Cass shone the lamplight on the man's face. No. He was no one Cass knew.

"It's Scott Torberg's father! He's the cook on the *Makepeace*," shouted Ansel. He put his ear over the man's heart.

Tongue began to lick the man's ears and neck. He licked him so hard across the nose and mouth that the body shifted and the head rolled.

The man opened his eyes and pushed Cass's lantern away. "Get that light out of my eyes!" he said.

Cass nearly fainted.

The man sat up and looked around. "*Uff da!*" he said, using the familiar Norwegian exclamation. "It's good to be on dry land."

"Come on. We'll get you to a fire," said Ansel.

"The ship's down below there, what's left of her," Torberg said wearily. "Two more men are trying to shinny up the brush on the side of the cliff."

"Where's the rest of the crew?" said Ansel.

"They got off in lifeboats an hour ago, when the engines quit and the power went out. The three of us were trapped."

"We've got a rope," said Cass. As Ansel lifted the coil over his head, Cass untied the stiff knot on his waist and tried to hand the rope to Torberg.

"I can't move my fingers," the man said. "I can't walk. You'll have to think of something. They're right below where I came up, clinging to a tree — unless they've been washed away."

Cass felt stunned. Torberg, who was supposed to be the grownup, had dumped the crisis in the boys' laps. Cass imagined the waves that blasted the cliff every few seconds. He strained to see the stunted pine they had passed and estimated its distance from the edge of the cliff. "Quick," he yelled to Ansel. "Tie your end to a loose rock. I've got an idea."

While Ansel went back toward the woods to find a rock, Cass wrapped his muffler around Torberg's bare foot, hoping it hadn't already frozen. After pushing and pulling the exhausted sailor to the shelter of the pine, he looped the rope around the tree trunk, low to the ground, leaving two long ends. One of these he tied around his own waist for a safety line. The other he would lower over the cliff, the edge of the world. And the rocks with their steepness, he thought, hoping that the pine roots had found a deep enough footing to hold.

He blessed Mun Benson for insisting that he learn to tie knots in the dark.

"Those men are needles in a haystack down there," said Cass. "I don't know where they are exactly. And with the waves drowning them, they'll never see the rope."

"Is your lantern waterproof?" asked Ansel, hefting the rock.

"No. It's just an ordinary lantern."

Cass remembered the anchor light in the pouch of his parka, and pulled it out. "But this is waterproof, and my dad says it's visible for two miles."

The Coast Guard required that all anchored boats display such a light to prevent collisions. It didn't cast a straight beam, but was visible from 360 degrees. Ansel turned it in his hands. "It'll break."

"No. It's made of some stuff they use in spaceships," said Cass. "I dropped it in the rocks at my house to test the guarantee. It got scuffed, and I had to replace a broken bulb, but you can see that it still shines."

"Let me have it." Ansel untied the rock and quickly attached the light to the end of the rope instead, using a knot unfamiliar to Cass.

To keep him out of the way, they tied Tongue to the stunted pine on which everything depended. While Ansel held the safety line taut, Cass flattened his body against the ground to gain as much friction as possible on the slick ice. He inched to the edge of the cliff where Torberg had been lying and the grinding of the ship's steel hull on the rocks was loudest.

For reassurance, he thought of Ansel, with heels dug in, one on each side of the tree, paying out safety line gradually and holding the excess looped around the trunk. Feeling the line around his waist and the knot pressing on his belly, he wished it strength.

He was awash in ice water. The crash against rock and the leap against gravity consumed the energy in the driven waves, Cass saw, and the wind dispersed the water. He wouldn't need a bath again soon.

He lowered the lantern over the slippery lip of the cliff and paid out rope from the coil he carried on his shoulder as he crawled.

With most of the coil still in his hands, the rope got hung up on something. On a ledge, maybe, or snagged in a tree. Or maybe good fortune and Saint Patrick's blessing had brought it straight into the hands of the men who needed it. Cass waited for a moment, wanting to waste no time, but afraid he would snatch the lifeline away from a man who could scarcely move his fingers.

He tugged twice on the rope and waited for a response. Nothing happened. He tried again. Still nothing. He pulled in the rope with as easy a touch as he could muster with freezing hands in sodden mittens, fearful that the light would smack against the rocks and shatter, despite the guarantee and the space-age materials. He hoped that Ansel knew how to tie knots that held.

When the rope came over the edge of the cliff, the light still shone.

Cass moved downshore a few feet, where the cliff projected slightly, and lowered the lantern again. The wind and spray yanked the rope like a salmon striking a lure, and every time, Cass's heart leaped.

He had heard of buck fever, the wobbly excitement that made greenhorn hunters feel faint when they spotted the deer they had been straining to see. Thinking that he was fishing for sailors, not salmon, that his quarry was men, not deer, Cass knew he could not afford the self-indulgence of buck fever. He made himself ignore the rope's jerking.

Ansel had said that the rope was fifty meters long. Cass figured that his own end, the safety line tied around his waist and looped around the tree, took about twenty-five feet. The distance from the tree to the cliff took another twenty-five feet off the lantern end of the rope. He remembered that the growth of heavy brush began about twenty feet above the normal water line. When he estimated that he had paid out thirty feet of rope over the side of the fifty-foot cliff, he stopped and waited for the sailors to come to the light.

Cass knew from his own forbidden adventures and near disasters on cliffs that it wouldn't be easy to scale that rock face on the calmest sunny day. The men would have to move from branch to branch, from tree to bush, feeling with numb feet for footholds on the rocks. If trapped himself between such a rock and such a hard place, Cass thought, he would try to stay on the back side of trees, where the branches would break the power of the water, offering some protection.

Now, forced to wait, Cass felt like an ant on the lip of the world. He thought of a poem his mother recited like a ghost story on snowbound winter nights: "Some say the world will end in fire, some say in ice." She could make him shiver when she spoke that poem.

Cass felt the menace of ice on his skin and bruised bones. His face ached, not only from the wind and water, but from the effort of squinting to protect his eyes. Shivers wracked his body. He began to plan for the moment soon when ice would force him to take refuge with fire. They would leave the lantern and the rope hanging as a beacon, a last hope.

But someone had pulled on the rope just then! Not the random snapping Cass had become used to, but a rhythmic signal that only a human could send. Cass signaled back and received a reply.

With the coil of rope around one arm, he crawled back to the tree.

"They've got it!" he shouted. "We found them! They've got the rope!"

Ansel passed the message on to Torberg, who was lying in the little shelter of the twisted pine, embracing Tongue, trying to warm his hands on the dog's body.

"He found them!" Ansel said. "They've got the rope."

Ansel and Cass took up all the slack in the lantern line and tied the taut rope to the pine trunk. Then they heaved together, wrapping the rope around their mittened hands and leaning back.

Torberg joined them, standing nearest the cliff and stronger even in his exhaustion than both boys together. As the rope came in, Cass kept tying the slack to the tree; if the sailors missed their footing and fell, the rope must not slip through the boys' hands.

Even with the aid of the rope, the climb up the cliff took a long time. But suddenly, there was the lantern, still lit, at the edge of the cliff, and above it, a man's face, glowing in the light. He crept toward them and collapsed in Torberg's arms.

"John!" said Torberg, searching the man's face. "Where's Kenny?"

Cass untangled the fisherman's knot tied next to the lantern at the man's waist. He raised the lamp.

"Lost," said John in a flat voice. "He couldn't hang on."

John's beard and mustache and his curly hair glistened, white with frost and frozen spray. The back of his khaki parka was caked with ice. "Lost," he said again. "One minute he was with me. The next time I looked, he was gone."

Both men sat down heavily. They leaned against the pine trunk, staring into space. Then, closing his eyes, John lay down on his side with his knees pulled up, hugging himself.

The boys looked at each other, astounded by the sailors' apathy. Without a thought, Cass had assumed when he saw adults that the men would take charge. Instead, they were falling asleep in a gale, soaked to the skin.

Furious, he shook the sailor's shoulder and shone the light in his eyes. "Wake up!" he shouted. "You can't go to sleep. You'll die."

"He's right, John," said Torberg. "We've got to get warm."

Ansel helped Torberg to his feet.

John tried to push Cass away. Grabbing a patch of bare skin on his cheek, Cass pinched as hard as he could.

"I've got a fire," he shouted in the sailor's ear. "Come on! You can do it. I'll help you."

Cass untied Tongue. He was a dog bred for retrieving ducks from icy water; nevertheless, despite his waterproof coat, he shivered uncontrollably. Cass let the dog go free, knowing he couldn't handle a leash and a half-drowned man besides, and trusting that Tongue would stay with him.

He jabbed John in the ribs with the ends of his stiff fingers, but his impatience got him nowhere.

Instead of crying, as he wanted to do, he made himself calm. On his knees, gently, he lifted the man's
shaggy head in both hands.

John opened his eyes. Cass looked straight into
them and spoke calmly, with authority. "Come with
me. I know what to do."

John struggled to his feet. Half skating, half
crawling, the boys guided the men back to the edge
of the woods, away from the frozen spray. All four
of them near collapse, holding each other up, they
followed Tongue into the wind, toward the cave.

Thirteen

Cass did know what to do.

The fire, fanned by the wind, had burned down to coals again by the time they crawled around it into the warm shelter. Cass gauged the woodpile and calculated that, by keeping the fire small, he could make it last several more hours.

"I've got some old clothes stashed in here that will fit you and me," Cass said to Ansel, nodding at the potato chip can.

He was shocked when Ansel replied, "I know. I saw them last summer."

There was no time now, though, to wonder about that.

Cass unzipped the goosedown sleeping bag and spread it out like a blanket across the broad floor of the cave. Opened flat, the sleeping bag was the size and shape of a double bed.

Ansel was helping John out of his wet clothes, with stiff fingers that couldn't grasp zippers and buttons.

"Here, Tongue." Cass dried the dog and coaxed him under the open sleeping bag. "This is a three-dog night, for sure, but one dog will have to do."

Answering the puzzled look on Torberg's face, Cass said, "I read that frontiersmen slept with dogs because their body temperature is higher than a human's. A three-dog night was a night so cold it took three dogs to keep a man warm."

"Tongue's a living electric blanket," said Torberg, smiling.

The men crawled between the sleeping bag and the canvas ground cloth, with their heads nearest the fire and Tongue shared between them. Already the dog had stopped shivering and settled himself for sleep. Cass hung the men's clothes on sticks and projecting rocks near the fire. Before long, he could smell the drying wool and leather.

Cass gave Ansel the long underwear and put on the spare pants and shirt himself. Ordinarily, he would have been embarrassed to change clothes with other people around, but after this night's dangers, he hardly noticed his own or the others' nakedness.

"Look," he said, pointing at bare wrists and ankles. "This stuff must have shrunk during the summer. I can't even fasten the pants. Or else I've grown."

"These are short," said Ansel, flexing his elbows and knees in the skimpy longjohns. "But at least they stretch."

Too exhausted for further talk, Cass switched off

the lantern. The two men and the two boys all curled up under the sleeping bag, trying to avoid kicking or crowding the others. Tongue groaned as the boys warmed their chilled feet on him.

"We'll have to line up feet to shoulder," said Torberg, "or we'll kick each other to death."

They all changed positions and settled down again. But everywhere Cass turned, a bruise or a scrape that he hadn't noticed before hurt. The bump on his head still throbbed, and bruises ached on his shins and hips. His windburned cheeks felt feverish.

Already Ansel was whistling through his nose and the men were snoring. But a whirl of drowsy thoughts troubled Cass. He imagined thrashing through the deep-drifted woods in the morning. The highway might even be drifted shut. He remembered the fire at school. That seemed long ago and unimportant now.

Would his parents punish him for running away? he wondered. How had they weathered the storm? Why had the cave not surprised Ansel, who even knew about the old clothes?

Cass yawned. All of that must wait until tomorrow. Overhead, the northeaster brawled, but the cave was warm; the fire fed with pine logs, snapped like static on a radio.

And fire with all the strength it hath, thought Cass. Silently he took comfort in his mother's blessing. Then, hoping Kenny had not fallen all the way down to the water, but had lodged in some tree, he drifted into sleep.

In the morning the gale still blew. It was a hum in the bones by now, an assumed presence in the world. So it was not the accustomed noise of the wind that woke Cass. Nor was it Torberg, who crouched at the mouth of the cave, fully dressed, rebuilding the burned-down fire.

Torberg cocked his head, listening for a sound that Cass had also heard on the wind.

"What is it?" asked Cass.

"We must be kidding ourselves," said Torberg. "I've been out there half a dozen times already. There's nothing."

John sat up abruptly. "How's your foot?"

Torberg held up his foot, neatly wound with Cass's fuzzy plaid scarf. "The frost took a little bite out of my toes. Nothing that won't cure, thanks to these boys and Tongue the Furnace."

Cass lit a candle.

"Solid ground never felt so good to a man," said John. "You boys are a couple of geniuses. I tell you, when I saw that lantern, I thought I was delirious. I thought you boys were the chariot, swinging low to carry me home."

They all laughed at the idea that, a few hours ago, John could have thought he was dying.

"How did you get off the ship onto the rocks?" said Ansel.

"The hull cracked when the ship struck the cliff," said John. "Torberg here scrambled up onto the tipped deck and ran into a spruce tree."

Torberg pointed to scratches on his cheeks.

"He took a flying leap into the dark," John went on, "and carried a rope across with him. Kenny and I monkey-crawled the rope."

There was an awkward silence when Kenny's name was mentioned.

Cass lay back, straining to hear the noise that had awakened him.

"We've got to get up to the road, Cass," said Torberg. "Maybe that noise we've been hearing is a snowplow."

"You can't walk on that foot; you'll freeze it again," said Ansel.

"I'll stay here, then, and you send someone for me."

On their knees, bumping into each other, John and the boys dressed as Torberg shook the clothes and handed them around. Cass gritted his teeth, pulling on his cold, damp jeans; his boots had baked so stiff in the heat from the fire that he could hardly lace them.

"Have you got any candy left?" said Ansel. "I've got a bear in my belly."

"How'd you know about the candy?" said Cass.

"And how'd you know about my cave and dry clothes?"

"This is *my* cave," said Ansel. "And this is my family's land."

Cass sat back on his heels and stared. "So that's where my supplies went."

"You just moved in like you owned the place," Ansel went on, "the same way you do everything. At first I was mad. Then I decided to spy on you and eat your food."

Ansel smiled in his old sneering way. "I saw you get ants in your pants. You never detected the master spy."

"You saw my moose?"

"She's *my* moose, creep. Her name is Bessie. She's lived in the cedars since she was a calf. We put a salt lick out for her."

"My dad said salt licks are illegal."

"Come off it, Cass. Quit being so high and mighty. If we don't shoot any of the game that comes to the lick, what harm can it do?"

"Other hunters might wait for her at the lick."

"That just shows how dumb you are, Cass. Everybody along the shore knows about Bessie and the lick. We keep city people off that land."

Ansel let his insult sink in. "We're good enough shots up here so we don't have to shoot my pet moose or other people's livestock to live."

Seeing the boys' growing anger, Tongue growled at Ansel. He bared his teeth, and the hair on his neck

116

stood on end. He took a protective stance in front of Cass.

"Hey!" said Torberg. "Don't kill each other till you're done saving us."

"Break out the grub, Cass," said John. "Seems to me, after a night like this, you heroes could go halves on the cave and split the moose down the middle. Come on. Did you save me from drowning to starve me to death?"

Cass had never been so thirsty, but he handed over the orange juice to the sailors. "This is all I've got left."

"Nah," said John. "Orange juice curdles my blood. What's six ounces of juice in a crowd like this, anyway? You boys drink it. I'll eat some snow."

Ansel broke up the chocolate from the potato chip can and offered it to the others.

"You'll need the energy to get to the road," said Torberg. "Share it."

"Listen!" said Cass.

This time the high-pitched whine in the distance was unmistakable. All together, they crowded out of the cave into the brighter daylight, where heavy snow still fell.

Cass squinted into the wind toward home, where he could hear a distant snowmobile. He began to run, but John chased after him and grabbed his parka.

"Hold your water. We've got to stick together. We're not out of the woods yet."

Cass strained to see. He could hear the snowmobile repeatedly come toward them a little and stop.

"It's your folks, out looking for you, Cass," said John.

The four survivors put their arms around each other and hollered. Three of them danced—all but Torberg, who pleaded, "For Pete's sake, don't step on my bad toes."

At last the snowmobile and driver emerged from the storm, close enough so Cass could see his father's face encircled in the frosted fur of his parka.

Cass hung back, relieved but nervous, too, as the snowmobile skidded to a stop and the others greeted Dad. Tongue leaped up, but Dad pushed him away and reached for Cass.

He raised the boy's chin with his hand and looked into his eyes. "Your mother's been looking for you all night," he said. "Where have you been?"

Uneasy with Dad's gaze boring into him, Cass looked away.

"He's been rescuing us, for one," said Torberg before Cass could answer. "We're off the *Makepeace*. She's on the rocks below."

"Anybody else make it?" asked Dad. Cass noticed that Dad's voice was hoarse, maybe from calling for him.

"One with us," said John. "We were trapped in the bow when the others got off in the boats. What do you hear of them?"

"Nothing," Dad said. "Munson Benson thought he saw a light east of his place last night, and the

Coast Guard picked up your radio signal. Mun's out on snowshoes looking for you." Dad glanced around the group. "What about the third man who was with you?"

"Kenny Schmidt," said John. "He fell. I'm afraid we've lost him."

"Your boys and this dog here saved us," said Torberg. "We'd never have made it up that cliff without them."

As the men talked, Dad held Cass with one arm tight around him. However Cass moved, he noticed, Dad's hand followed, as if it were stuck to his shoulder. He felt Dad patting him and gently stroking his arm. Yet Cass could not jump the gulf he felt between them and return Dad's affection.

"How did you make it through the night?" Dad asked, turning back to him.

Fear of Dad's anger and disappointment filled his throat. As he hesitated, Ansel replied for him. "We slept in a cave Cass and I knew about, around behind these rocks."

Bending to look into the mouth of the cave, Dad said, "So that's where you stashed all that food and gear last summer."

He stood erect again and gathered his authority as if inhaling air after a long time underwater. "Now to find Kenny and the other crewmen. Can you fellows hold out for a while longer? Ansel's folks are frantic about him. I'll take him up to Petersons' and get a search party together."

"I don't want to go home until we've found Kenny," said Ansel.

"Take Torberg," said John. "His foot's froze. The boys and I need to see this through. Maybe Kenny's stuck in a tree down there. A little food wouldn't hurt though, when you come back. And some dry clothes."

Cass felt that he must speak to Dad or explode. "There was a fire at school," he said. "Are you going to ground me, Dad?" Though stung by the pelting snow as he squinted into the wind, he met his father's eyes.

Dad shook his head impatiently. "I read your note, but I couldn't believe it. Is that fire the whole story behind this awful night?"

Cass looked at his feet, unable to reply.

"Mr. Ulseth straightened out the misunderstanding before you got off the schoolbus."

"You mean I didn't even have to run away?"

"Nothing you could do is so bad you'd have to do that, Cass." Dad gently touched his face and tried to hug him, but Cass squirmed out of reach.

"It's a lucky thing you were here in a safe place last night," Dad continued in an ironic, joking tone, "and not taking chances in Cabin 1. The water never touched it in fifty years. But last night Lake Superior ate it in one gulp."

Cass couldn't believe his ears, but Dad had more to tell. "She's gone — beds, refrigerator, bottled gas

120

and all. This morning, there's just an empty space where the cabin used to stand. All we found was the toaster and a lampshade, tossed up on the lawn."

Dad shuddered. "Mom and I were afraid you might have hidden out there after dark," he whispered.

Cass imagined himself, snatched from sleep in Cabin 1, bobsledding down the troughs of waves aboard the old iron bedstead, flying over the crests with a sheet for a sail. He was dizzy with hunger and fatigue and shock.

"Mom's all right? Eileen?" Cass was afraid of the answer.

"They will be, when they know you're safe," said Dad. "This will be the best Thanksgiving we ever had."

Cass felt as if a mountain had been lifted from his back. He looked up at his father's haggard face, with its silvery stubble of beard and black wells encircling bloodshot eyes.

"I love you, Cass," said Dad quietly. "You're everything I always hoped you'd be."

Cass threw his arms around his father. They leaned against each other in an embrace that kept them standing despite their shaky legs. Then Dad took a deep breath and turned back to the group. "Ready, Torberg?"

Standing with John and Ansel, Cass silently watched Torberg and Dad climb aboard the snowmobile and fade into the blizzard. Then the three of them crawled back into the shelter of the cave and lay down for a long time, quiet in the dim light. Tongue settled himself with a groan. Cass felt used up. His mind wandered, and he fell into a drowsy dream of summer.

"When the weather clears," said Ansel at last, "do you think our folks will let us camp out here some weekend?"

"I don't see why not. After last night, the rest of our lives will be easy," said Cass. He turned his head and looked at Ansel. "Next time, though, you bring the food."